A PUERTO RICAN
in New York and
OTHER SKETCHES

JESUS COLON

A PUERTO RICAN
in New York and
OTHER SKETCHES

INTERNATIONAL PUBLISHERS, NEW YORK

Library of Congress Cataloging in Publication Data
Colon, Jesus, 1901-1974
    A Puerto Rican in New York, and other sketches.

    1. Puerto Ricans—New York (N.Y.) 2. New York
(N.Y.)—Social life and customs. 3. Colon, Jesus,
1901-1974.   I. Title.
F128.9.P85C64 1982   305.8'687295'07471   82-6100
ISBN 0-7178-0589-1 (pbk.)   AACR2

Contents

Contents

Illustrations by Ernesto Ramos Nieves who is gratefully aware that their realization owes much to the support and criticism of Lourdes, a Puerto Rican woman in New York.

Foreword

When Jesus Colon stowed away to New York back in 1918, most of the Puerto Ricans leaving San Juan for the United States were artisans. There were of course many unskilled workers, and a sprinkling of professionals and business people, but for the most part those early emigrants were carpenters, bakers, bricklayers, house painters, typesetters. The core of these artisan contingents, though, consisted of *tabaqueros*, young apprenticed cigarmakers headed for jobs in the countless small cigar factories in New York, Miami, and other East Coast cities.

The cigar workers—men and women—often came with more than just their trade. They were also remarkably educated, having been reared among that most militant and intellectually enlightened sector of the Puerto Rican working class. In Puerto Rico as in many other Caribbean and Latin American countries, the *tabaqueros* and other artisans formed the political leadership and organizational backbone of the entire labor movement. Since the turn of the century in Puerto Rico, they had been instrumental in the growth and strategy of the *Federación Libre de Trabajadores*, and were vocal participants at the founding of the Socialist Party in 1915 in Cayey, the very town where Colon was born and raised.

The voices Jesus Colon heard through his window while still a boy and recalls here in the opening sketch, might well have been from that historic gathering. They were the voices of the *lectores* who would come to the factories every day to read aloud from newspapers and books as the workers sat rolling cigars. Colon was schooled in the class struggle, his first teachers being the *tabaqueros* and other working-class leaders from all over Puerto Rico championing the cause of proletarian revolution and international solidarity. In 1917, just before Colon departed for New York, those organized and class-conscious

workers represented the only voice in Puerto Rican politics to hail the
victory of the Bolshevik Revolution.

Such were the ideals that many of the early Puerto Rican emigrants
brought with them as they arrived and struck roots, however reluc-
tantly, in New York. Jesus Colon was thus representative of that first
large-scale influx from the Island, as was Bernardo Vega, a young
tabaquero (from Cayey!) who made the trek in the same years and
who was also to record his life in New York decades later, at mid-
century. *A Puerto Rican in New York* and Bernardo Vega's memoirs
(Memorias de Bernardo Vega) are in fact unique documents of their
kind, offering the only sustained glimpses we have of the New York
Puerto Rican community during the decades prior to 1950. Here we
get a sense of what motivated Puerto Ricans to set out en masse in the
first place, who those pioneering families were, and what it was like
for them upon landing and seeking out a new life in this bulging
metropolis. We witness first-hand the fantasy-world New York,
known to them from illustrated magazines and picture postcards,
dashing against the somber reality of the crowded tenements where
they came to live, while their prospects for stable employment
dwindled the longer they stayed. We also learn how, after the initial
fits and starts, the community began forming organizations to provide
for the needed cultural cohesion and a political voice in these unfamiliar and often hostile surroundings. And, finally, these documents
tell of the Puerto Ricans' initial relations with their new-found neighbors, the multitude of other immigrant nationalities in the touted
"melting pot" who, like themselves, had come from foreign shores in
search of a brighter future.

Like Colon and Vega, the majority of those *tabaqueros* and other
workers who migrated in the early decades ended up staying in New
York, as their nagging hope to return to the Island drifted ever further
into the future. The critical convictions many of them had gained in
childhood from the social struggles back home were only reinforced
by the long lives of hardship and resistance they were to endure in the
land of opportunity. In New York they came to understand even more
clearly the international dimension of the struggle against that very

system of imperialism which held their beloved Puerto Rico in direct colonial bondage, the same system that was ultimately responsible for their own "decision" to leave their homeland behind.

Through the decades this vantage point was to inform their energetic activity in the political life of the New York Puerto Rican community. In the Spanish and English-language newspapers, the patriotic and workers' organizations, at civic, cultural, and religious occasions, it was the *tabaquero* emigrants who most effectively promoted unity among Puerto Ricans in standing up to the rampant discrimination and chronic injustice levelled against them. It was the likes of Jesus Colon, too, who consistently and correctly ascribed the disadvantaged position of his uprooted countrymen in the United States to the enduring colonial status of the Island. The Puerto Ricans' battle for equality in New York had to be tied at every point to the cause of independence for the Puerto Rican nation.

At the same time they recognized that for working-class emigrants from a direct colonial nation, the ruling circles of which were long committed to maintaining imperialism and mass migration, the goal of internal unity was clearly not adequate, and could in fact be seriously misleading. In the new battleground of the North American cities, Puerto Rican workers need allies, and they have readily found them among the people with whom they work and live. At first, in the *tabaquero* days, it was the Cubans: the books by Jesus Colon and Bernardo Vega, taking up where the late nineteenth-century writings of Hostos, Betances, and "Pachin" Marin left off, bear further testimony to the ongoing history of solidarity between Puerto Ricans and Cubans in New York. Most pronounced during those years of unified struggle against Spain, this tradition remained intense and practical during the teens and twenties, when they came to work in the same cigar factories, fight in the same unions, and live in the same rooming houses.

But the Caribbean *tabaqueros'* ideals were to stand the test of time more successfully than was their ill-fated trade. During World War I, as they poured in by shiploads, the cigar industry was already entering its final decline. The cigarmakers—Puerto Rican and Cuban alike—

were within a decade nudged out of their inherited place in the labor
force through the combined pressure of mechanization, commercial
monopolies, and the advent of the cigarette. By the mid-1920s, pos-
sessing an obsolete skill and no means to return home, the early
emigrants were set adrift in the North American working class, taking
up what jobs and housing there were alongside of immigrant Italians,
Irish, Jews and Latin Americans of various nationalities, and American
Blacks. (Jesus Colon himself was to spend his years in New York as a
dishwasher, dockworker, postal clerk, and at dozens of other menial
posts. That is, when he wasn't working at looking for work, as in stories
like "Easy Job, Good Wages" and "Kipling and I," or engaged full-
time at political organizing).

Racial prejudice in the United States made immediately and abun-
dantly clear to Puerto Ricans, especially black Puerto Ricans like Jesus
Colon and Arturo Alfonso Schomburg, that it is the minority groups—
Chicanos, Native Americans, Asians, and particularly the Afro-Amer-
ican people—that constitute their most immediate historical allies in
the United States. Yet the bond between them, like the unity among
workers of Caribbean and Latin American origins, is based on class
and politics, not race, and of necessity extends to workers and
progressive people of all backgrounds. Which is why Jesus Colon,
writing in the 1950s, could declare with such confidence that the
"American idol" of Puerto Ricans "was and still is Vito Marcantonio."
And to think, as Colon noted in his preface, that those were the very
years when the hostility between Puerto Ricans and Italians were
being displayed to the world in all the appealing glamour of a hit
Broadway musical, *West Side Story*, which has left its indelible
imprint on the popular image—and self-image—of Puerto Ricans in
the United States ever since.

Recognizing that their prospects called for utmost class solidarity,
many Puerto Rican workers in New York turned to the Communist
movement, and Colon again was no exception. He was an active,
articulate member of the Communist Party through the Depression
years, World War II, and McCarthyism, and remained so until the end
of his life in 1974. Over the years he was also involved in dozens of

political, civic, and cultural organizations, holding responsible and influential positions in the International Workers Order and the American Labor Party.

Jesus Colon would agree with Bernardo Vega, who wrote toward the end of his *Memorias,* "Siempre es más interesante vivir que escribir." ("It is always more interesting to live than to write."). Like Bernardo, he was a man of action, whose political efforts were always tied intimately to his direct association with friends, neighbors, and fellow workers. Yet, through the years he always seemed to find time to write. In the 1920s he was a regular New York contributor to the socialist newspapers in Puerto Rico, *Justicia* and *Unión Obrera.* He also wrote occasional poems, anecdotes, and articles for *El Machete Criollo, El Nuevo Mundo* and Bernardo Vega's weekly, *Gráfico,* all published in New York. Through the 1930s and into the 1950s he contributed frequently to *The Daily Worker, The Worker* and *Mainstream.* In the late 1940s he wrote prolifically for the weekly *Liberación,* little known today but in its time the main New York forum for progressive writers from Spain, Cuba, Puerto Rico, and other Latin American countries. Founded in 1946 as an anti-Franco organ, *Liberación* quickly expanded its scope and until it ceased publication in 1949, gave full voice to the Cuban and Puerto Rican liberation struggles. Colon himself contributed lengthy articles analyzing the rapidly expanding migration and the changing political position of Puerto Ricans in New York. Other Puerto Rican journalists and authors to write for *Liberación* included José Luis González, Bernardo Vega, Clemente Soto-Vélez, César Andreu Iglesias, and Guillermo Cotto-Thorner.

Most of *A Puerto Rican in New York* was written in the years immediately following. By mid-century, the Puerto Rican migration to New York was reaching proportions never before imagined by Colon and the other contributors to *Liberación.* Puerto Ricans were flooding in by air now, and not by the hundreds but by the tens of thousands. And there was no sign that this avalanche, unleashed in the 1940s as part of the infamous development plan for Puerto Rico, "Operation Bootstrap," would soon subside. As more workers were leaving the Island than finding employment there, interest in the "Puerto Rican problem" in New York became more intense—and more hysterical—than ever. The brutal campaign of oppression against the Nationalist Party and the independence movement was but one of the more prominent signs of this reaction against the colonial newcomers.

It was in the 1950s, too, and largely in response to these rapidly changing conditions, that there emerged an actual literature of the Puerto Rican emigrant community. Puerto Rican writers, from the Island and those living in New York, turned their attention to lending fictional representation to the migration and resettlement experience. Puerto Rican life in New York, previously the subject of journalism, autobiographical anecdotes, and popular tunes, now became the setting and thematic focus of novels, stories, and plays. José Luis González' *El hombre en la calle*, René Marqués' *La carreta*, Guillermo Cotto-Thorner's *Trópico en Manhattan*, Bernardo's *Memorias*, and Pedro Juan Soto's *Spiks* were all written in the late 1940s and early 1950s. In all of them, as in Colon's stories, the Puerto Rican emigrant is the collective protagonist, and his encounter with the New York setting the center of narrative and dramatic attention. These works also share a preoccupation with the lot of common people, a sense of estrangement and frustration in the cold, northern surroundings, and a posture of defiant resistance and self-affirmation in the face of severe adversity. While there is some range of emotional emphasis and stylistic features, these writings all betray evident influences of Hemingway, Steinbeck and Wilder. Most important, they are alike in striving to capture the existential predicament of their characters realistically, in social and historical terms. To this extent, *A Puerto Rican in New York* is unmistakably part of its literary generation, the best of the sketches having their rightful place alongside those masterful stories by González, Soto and others.

What most obviously distinguishes Jesus Colon's "sketches" among the stories and scenes from the 1950s, however, is that they were written in English. *A Puerto Rican in New York*, it seems, was the first book-length literary or semiliterary treatment of the subject to appear in English. Not that Colon abandoned Spanish or meant to suggest any preference for English: he continued to write and carry out much of his activity in his native tongue. Needless to say, he was always a staunch upholder of the right of Puerto Ricans and other Hispanic people to participate in North American society free of prejudice because of their language background.

But his choice to draft his only book in English was a significant one: more than an issue of language, it signals deeper differences with his literary peers of the 1950s, as well as an anticipation of the New York-based Puerto Rican literature of the ensuing decades. For most of those Spanish-language renderings of Puerto Rican experience in New York were composed, as it were, from the outside and in transition; as is clear from the works themselves, their authors were only in the United States on relatively short stays during which they gathered the flavor and tempo of their fictional settings. Typically, the overriding experience of their characters in the New York environment is alienation, exclusion and traumatic desperation, an anguished culture-shock leading inevitably to existential nostalgia for the Island. Even Bernardo Vega and Cotto-Thomer, though like Colon they spent all of their adult lives in New York, still present the emigrant colony as largely self-contained, and to be understood primarily in reference to Puerto Rico. This is not to detract from the literary quality or historical accuracy of these works, but only to account for their general thematic orientation.

Jesus Colon, by contrast, was writing of Puerto Ricans who were in New York to stay, and whose life-drama came to hinge less on their sense of contrast with the Island than on their individual and collective interaction with North American society and the workers of diverse cultures with whom they were coming into increasing contact. The simple English prose of *A Puerto Rican in New York* takes us beyond the novelty of arrival and its lingering aftermath to the Puerto Ricans digging in and taking stock of their altered historical situation in its own right. Colon shows how non-Puerto Ricans inhabit and play influential roles in this new terrain of Puerto Rican reality. Yet he is also intent on making the story of his people accessible and comprehensi-

ble to the broad non-Hispanic readership in the United States
and internationally.

His "sketches," therefore, break more than the language bar-
rier; they aim to chip away at the formidable wall of stereotypes
and bigotry which has long shrouded the image of all Puerto
Ricans in the public eye. Not the least damaging of these self-
fulfilling myths about Puerto Ricans is their very "isolation,"
their supposed inability or unwillingness to relate to others.
How movingly and resolutely Colon undermines such obstacles
through characters like Sarah, José, Marcelino, and the lady who
lived near the statue of a man on a horse. For these are stories
of Puerto Ricans in constant and mutually rewarding involve-
ments with working people of many nationalities, and exhibiting
those qualities of pride and modesty, friendly hospitality and
hatred of injustice with which North American people of all backgrounds can readily sympathize and identify. It is with the same
strategic irony that Colon, a life-long Communist and fighter for
Puerto Rican independence, appropriates the familiar terms of
the U.S. Constitution to frame his vision of equality and freedom.

With this focus on Puerto Ricans fully caught up in the dy-
namic of U. S. society, Colon's stories foreshadow the vibrant
literature of the "Nuyoricans" that has emerged since the late
1960s. Many of these young writers may not be familiar with *A
Puerto Rican in New York*, and they are of course separated from
the earlier decades by a flurry of intervening events. The 1960s
saw a sharp ebb in Puerto Rican emigration followed by large-
scale return migration during the 1970s; in 1959 just after Colon
completed his book, came the Cuban Revolution; these events
along with the impact of the Civil Rights and Black Power movements, the Vietnam War and its opposition have altered signifi-
cantly the character of the Puerto Rican community. The new
writing, in fact, forms part of an embracing cultural and political
resurgence among Puerto Ricans born and raised here. It represents the literary generation since the 1950s, chroniclers of the
Puerto Rican experience who express themselves in English—and
bilingually—not so much out of political choice but because it is
their spontaneous means of verbal interaction and creativity.

But despite these differences, Piri Thomas, Nicholasa Mohr, Tato Laviera and Sandra Maria Esteves, to name a few, are carrying forward traditions introduced by Jesus Colon. The human scenes and predicaments of Puerto Rican immigrant life sketched in simple lines by Colon in the 1950s are being elaborated in striking tones and increasingly complex linguistic and psychological dimensions by the writers of the present generation. And, from all indications, Colon's intellectual and literary legacy will continue to guide Puerto Ricans in what promise to be even more ominous and trying times ahead.

Beyond that, his images of friendship and human solidarity, bis steady grasp of the relation between colonial and working-class that transcends the particularity of their case. As a result, *A Puerto Rican in New York* makes invaluable reading for anyone who would gain a closer understanding of labor and immigrant history, ethnic and racial relations, and the centrality of Caribbean-U.S. affairs in the present-day workings of world imperialism. Jesus Colon throws open a window through which all can hear an intelligible and sympathetic Puerto Rican voice.

June, 1982   JUAN FLORES
Centro de estudios puertorriqueños
(CUNY)

To the memory of
CONCHA

A PUERTO RICAN
in New York and
OTHER SKETCHES

Preface

Very little has been written about the Puerto Rican in New York City.

True, one may find voluminous studies and official reports in almost all the city's departments but, on the one hand, these documents generally reduce the Puerto Ricans to statistical ups and downs on municipal charts, or, on the other, they are often left to gather dust in the archives.

Then, some readers may have read one or another of the periodic series on "The Puerto Rican Problem" that keep recurring in the New York press, from the *Long Island Newsday* to *The New York Times*. Even magazines like *Fortune, Harper's* and *The New Yorker* have found it expedient on occasion to provide their readers with elaborate highly-documented "surveys" of the "difficult" problem of the "unwanted, unassimilable Puerto Ricans" who live in the great metropolis of New York and other large industrial cities.

We Puerto Ricans have even been subjected to treatment in the Broadway drama and a fabulously successful musical show. But invariably this treatment harps on what is superficial and sentimental, transient and ephemeral, or bizarre and grotesque in Puerto Rican life—and always out of context with the real history, culture and traditions of my people.

Circulation executives demand cheap sensationalism in their newspaper and magazine features about the Puerto Rican community. The ticket-buying public is lured to shows on the basis of the "jungle" character of plays and performers. Books are promoted to the best-seller lists baited with shock and shudder, with lurid depictions of unbridled violence and terror in the daily conduct of these "new-comers" to our fair city.

Years ago, it was the "brutal and uncouth" Irish; then it was the "knife-wielding" Italians; later it was the "clannish" Jews

9

with "strange" ways; yesterday it was the Negro; today, it is the Puerto Ricans—and the Negroes—who are relegated to the last rung of New York's social ladder.

So the Puerto Ricans—over half a million of us!—remain unsung, unheralded and practically unknown to their fellow New Yorkers, except through the filter of an assiduously cultivated hostility, distrust and ignorance.

Not one of the statistical studies and dramatic presentations conveys the slightest idea of the significant historical heritage of the Puerto Rican people or of the Puerto Ricans' contributions to the cultural advancement of the Western hemisphere, including that of the United States. There is no inkling of our international outlook, our solidarity with the struggles of other peoples, especially our sense of identity with the peoples of Latin America. There is no hint of the deep traditions of striving for freedom and progress that pervade our daily life.

The sketches that follow are a modest attempt by a Puerto Rican who has lived in New York many years—always among his own people—through the medium of personal experience to throw a little light on how Puerto Ricans in this city *really* feel, think, work and live.

A number of these sketches and vignettes appeared in *The Worker*, some in *Mainstream*, some abroad, but most have never been published before. Had it not been for the incentive of the many warm and friendly letters from readers all over the country, some in praise, some in criticism, but always encouraging, most of these sketches would not have been written.

To each of these letter-writers—a red rose.

JESUS COLON

1. A Voice Through the Window

When I was a boy in Cayey, my hometown in Puerto Rico, we lived in a house in back of which was a big cigar factory. Every morning, starting around ten, a clear, strong voice coming from the big factory came through my window. It had a tinge of the oratorical in it.

One morning my boyish curiosity was aroused beyond endurance. I went through the backyard to one of the ground floor windows of the cigar factory. There were about one hundred and fifty cigarmakers, each one sitting in front of tables that looked like old-fashioned rolltop desks, covered with all kinds of tobacco leaves. The cigarmakers with their heads bent over their work listened intently. In the vast hall of the factory, I looked for the source of the voice to which they were listening. There was a man sitting on a chair on a platform. The platform had a thin wooden railing around it, except for the opening where a short, steep and narrow wooden staircase connected the platform with the floor below.

Later, upon inquiring, I came to know that the man up on the platform was responsible for the clear, strong voice. He was called "El Lector"—the Reader. His job was to read to the cigarmakers while they were rolling cigars. The workers paid fifteen to twenty-five cents per week each to the reader. In the morning, the reader used to read the daily paper and some working class weeklies or monthlies that were published or received from abroad. In the afternoon he would read from a novel by Zola, Balzac, Hugo, or from a book by Kropotkin, Malatesta or Karl Marx. Famous speeches like Castelar's or Spanish classical novels like Cervantes' *Don Quixote* were also read aloud by "El Lector."

So you were amazed by the phenomenon of cigarmakers who hardly knew how to read and write, discussing books like Zola's *Germinal,* Balzac's *Pere Goriot,* or Kropotkin's *Fields, Factories and Workshops,* during the mild Puerto Rican evenings in the public square.

11

Yes, the Reader was a very important person in the cigar factory and in the general life of the cigarmakers. He was usually something of an orator and an actor ready to strike a pose at the least provocation. So through my early boyhood this voice of the Reader, coming defiant and resonant from the cigar factory through my window, used to enchant and instruct me in the style of these great French and Spanish novelists and the ideas of their various schools of thought. Frankly speaking, at that tender age I rather preferred the straight stories of Zola or Balzac to the ideological architecture of the thinkers, most of whose concepts went over my head.

But one thing is certain, my ear got accustomed to hearing the repetition of certain words and phrases which, as I grew up, I came to understand more clearly.

Sometimes, when I am in a meditative mood, I just close my eyes and isolate myself from my surroundings. Then I transport myself to my childhood in Puerto Rico. I can see that window and listen to that voice reading from the adventures of Don Quixote or the miseries and persecution suffered by Jean Valjean, books and characters that will be remembered many years after the latest "whodunit" has been read and forgotten.

The Cigar Factory Reader was something more. He was usually connected with the socialist movement. He was the town orator for the baptismal parties, weddings, ceremonies or eulogies when death took away one of the more or less prominent persons in the town. Sometimes the Reader joined the cigarmakers' conversations at one of the benches in the public square. On such occasions, everybody was waiting for any pearl of wisdom that might drop from his mouth. This would be favorably compared with the latest harangue from our town mayor or the sermon of last Sunday given by the priest at the Catholic church with the rose-colored dome, where most of us had been baptized.

Some of these readers became very famous throughout the cigar-manufacturing towns of Puerto Rico. There was one who at the very end of the day's work used to close the book he was reading and continue to "read" from memory to the workers. Some of the cigarmakers had taken the trouble of bringing a copy of the book to work in order to follow the reader from his closed book just to see if he left something out. The reader never did. These feats of memory encouraged many workers and even boys like myself to try memorizing well-known passages like the introductory paragraph of *Don Quixote,* with which we started to like and then to love literature and the enlightened thinkers of mankind.

I still hear this voice through the window of my childhood. Sometimes I listen to the same themes today. Sometimes in Spanish, most of the time in English, from the halls and squares of this New York of ours. Sometimes this voice comes through the radio, from Europe and Asia, crystallized now in pamphlets and books that have shaken the world to its foundations. But always the theme is the same, the same as the readers from the cigarmaker's factory, coming to my home in my childhood's past.

Always the same voice of the reader of my boyhood memories. But now clearer, stronger, surer, devoid of rhetoric, based on facts and history.

This voice seems to be saying now, as it said through the reader's mouth in my distant childhood: The confusions, misunderstandings, disillusions, defections and momentary defeats will be overcome. In the end, if we keep on struggling and learning from struggle, the workers and their allies will win all over the world.

2. My First Literary Venture

Mercedes was one of the girls in my 8th grade class in grammar school at San Juan, Puerto Rico. When you say about a girl that she looked like an angel, you must have Mercedes in mind.

One day Mercedes did not come to class. Word was sent to the school principal that Mercedes' mother had died. The principal came into our classroom. Our teacher abruptly finished what she was saying and silently stepped aside as all teachers do when their "superiors" come into their room. "Mercedes' mother died this morning," the principal said. The forty of us, girls and boys, were all ears. We thought that she would go into details as to the kind of sickness that had caused the death of Mercedes' mother. But the principal instead wanted to explain another matter to us. "We should like to express to Mercedes and her family the condolence that we all feel towards her loss." Here she paused for a long time before she continued. "This is not for your teacher or for me to do as individuals. We must write a letter to Mercedes and her family in which the whole feeling of this class is reflected." She then finished with the following words: "All of you, individually, are going to write a letter to Mercedes in the name of myself, your teacher and this class. The one letter that in the opinion of your teacher and myself best conveys the sympathy and emotions of all of us will be the one we will send to Mercedes' family."

The letter I wrote had just three short paragraphs. This was the one selected.

3. My First Strike

The building used by the grammar school had been a military armory during the time the Spanish government occupied Puerto Rico. The long dark hallways were lined with stuffed birds, monkeys and other animals in dusty glass cages waiting for a more suitable place to show themselves to the general public.

Good old Central Grammar School at San Francisco and Luna Streets, right in the heart of San Juan, Puerto Rico!

Our room was Number 12, famous because its class had the best and the worst boys and girls in all the schools. The best athletes, the most promising incipient poets and writers, the ones always ready for a fight or a boy's prank at the least insinuation. Many from the class of Room 12 are today prominent in Puerto Rican letters, science and jurisprudence.

Our teacher in American History was Mr. Whole, a tall Montanan, always with a deceptive grin on his face. One day, at the end of the class, a girl informed the teacher that her history text book had disappeared from her desk. Mr. Whole asked if anyone had seen the girl's book. Then, after a pause, he asked if anyone had taken the girl's book. There was no answer. After a long silence, Mr. Whole said: "If nobody knows where the book is and nobody has taken the book, the price of the book will have to be divided among all of you, as it has to be replaced to the school. It will amount to about ten cents per student. Everybody shall bring ten cents tomorrow; otherwise he or she will not be allowed to come into the room."

Next day, as the students started to come to school, all the boys and girls of Room 12 gathered instinctively around one of the benches on the public square facing the school. Then and there we decided that we were not going in that day. A committee of three was elected to see the school principal and present our demands. I was elected Chairman of the Committee.

15

We waited until all the classes but ours were sitting in their rooms. Not one student appeared in Mr. Whole's class. We were watching every move. From the square we could see everything inside through the school windows. We saw when Mr. Whole, tired of waiting for us, entered the school principal's office. I presented the case very concisely in the name of the committee and of our school class. I finished by saying that it was unjust for Mr. Whole to tax us ten cents apiece for something in which we felt we were blameless. We finished by saying very emphatically that the class refused to come in until Mr. Whole rescinded the ten cent order.

After some argument with the Principal and with us, Mr. Whole agreed to rescind the order.

The strike was won.

4. The Way To Learn

After the school authorities in San Juan, Puerto Rico, condemned the old Spanish soldiers barracks, between San Francisco and Luna Streets, corner Tanca, so that they could build a new school building on its site, they placed all of us in some makeshift wooden barracks near the seashore, in the picturesque capital district called "Puerta de Tierra."

We called our new quarters, which passed for a school, "Barracones" (big barracks). We had classes here, from 6th grade grammar school to the second year of high school. We managed to have one of the best baseball teams in the San Juan school district; and we had our own school magazine. Its name was "Adelante!" (Forward).

In a very democratic election, in which practically everybody in Barracones expressed his opinion, a Board was elected for our magazine "Adelante." This happened around 1917 . . . And what a Board those boys and girls elected! It really made you swear by the effectiveness of the democratic process. How good, mentally clean and unspoiled and talented they were, even if I have to say so myself—for I was elected editor of "Adelante."

Today, I dare say that none of us are as good, as true, and as sincere as we were when we served on that editorial board. Last heard from, one was pensioned off from the Puerto Rican government, another became the editor of an important daily paper in Puerto Rico's second largest city, another is or was the President of Puerto Rico's Lawyer's Association and still another is the President of the General Confederation of Labor of Puerto Rico, and one of the two delegates from Puerto Rico at the CIO-AFL merger convention. And I, the humblest of the humble, and the proudest of the proud, writing my column from my old battered desk in the office of the American "Daily Worker"—the greatest honor I feel a writer could ever aspire to in these United States.

But let us go back to Barracones, near the sea in the Puerta de Tierra district of the capital city of San Juan Puerto Rico. Puerta de Tierra had something in those days for which it was justly famous. Its fighting militant women—mostly wives of dock workers.

On every mobilization by the workers for a meeting, or a parade, you could count on the dock workers' wives living in "Puerta de Tierra." For a strike—especially a dock workers' strike—the women of "Puerta de Tierra" would go out in a body, shouting the strikers' demands all over San Juan.

All the boys and girls in the school of Barracones will remember particularly one of those dock workers' strikes in "Puerta de Tierra." We were all out in the school yard after our lunch hour, as the parade of striking dock workers was passing by. Parades and public demonstrations were absolutely forbidden during this strike period. The shipowners and the police were very concerned at the growing effectiveness of the strikers' parades. Mounted police with carbines ready for any emergency were patrolling the workers' districts of the capital. Puerto de Tierra was one of these districts.

As the parade of workers and their wives marched down the street, we saw about a dozen mounted policemen coming from the opposite direction. The parade continued on, with slogans and union banners flying.

As the mounted police saw the parade formation coming towards them, they lined up on their large, strong horses, into an impassable fortress from one side of the street to the other.

There was a moment of suspense and indecision on the part of the workers—it might have been fifteen seconds or more. To us boys and girls, with our heads between the fence slats, these seconds of hesitancy were like an eternity.

At last, taking two steps forward, one of the strikers holding a banner began to march forward and sing at the same time:

*Arriba los pobres del mundo
De pie los esclavos sin pan

He continued marching with head up toward the mounted police. The rest of the strikers with their wives and their sisters followed after him.

The one in charge of the mounted platoon gave a signal, so imperceptible that nobody seemed to notice. The police moved as if by a spring, moving their carbines to their shoulders and taking aim. It was done rapidly, but coolly, calmly, dispassionately. It seems to me as if I can see them right now. Another almost imperceptible signal and all of them shot at the same time. The worker with the banner was the first to fall pierced by the police bullets.

But a strange thing happened—the strikers and their supporters continued marching forward until strikers, horses, women, children and police were in a whirling mass of fighting humanity. Women started stabbing the underbelly of the horses with long hat pins until the horses, frightened by the uproar and in pain threw the riders from their backs into the fighting multitude.

The strikers kept on pushing, singing and fighting the police. The brutal initial coldblooded shooting by the representatives of "law and order" seemed to have incensed them to a fury.

One of the policemen managed to mount his horse. He started to ride toward the center of the city evidently for reinforcements. Some of the workers noticed the maneuver. As if by an invisible language known only to the initiated, the word was passed around as they continued to bang the heads, bodies and legs of the remaining policemen.

A few minutes later the street was deserted. Half a dozen workers, making a human stretcher of their hands and arms woven together, took the body of their dead companion away. Only old caps, dirty ties, pieces of shirts and old sneakers were

---

*The Internationale in Spanish. This was one of the many socialist versions:

Arise, ye prisoners of starvation
Arise, you wretched of the earth.

spread all over as the tragic reminders of what took place a few minutes before.

Our young heads remained "glued" between the slats of the school fence. The school bell woke us to the reality of classes. In fact, the principal rang the bell far in advance of the accustomed time, in an unsuccessful effort to return all of us to our classrooms . . . all in vain.

In our next issue of *Adelante*, our school paper, a whole review of that murderous attack on the workers appeared. It read:

Honest Struggle of Our Parents

On Friday March 23rd at the critical hour of going to school, a controversy between policemen and strikers originated beside the public school. The danger which we were in was immense.

The policemen's bullets dropped like rain on the defenseless multitudes.

As the strikers saw themselves being attacked in such a manner, they started to use their only defense arms: the stones in the street. With them they faced the wanton fire of the policemen. An outstanding deed of that tragic hour of desolation and death, of sadness and terror, came as a climax in front of *four hundred school children.*

A herculean man, of athletic form, young, a peaceful lover of labor and an indefatigable fighter for his daily bread, tumbled lifeless right on the street in a just struggle for bread for work and for collective equality.

Right in front of a school, before four hundred school children! What an example of *culture and philanthropy!*

Abel's blood does not call us to justice any more; Christ's prophetic words no longer console the weak; God's eyes don't watch over us anymore.

In no page of our history has a deed of such magnitude ever been registered!

Our dear fathers struggle for bread but they fall vanquished, covered with blood! Oh, formidable struggle! Oh, endless struggle, with stupid political bossism backed up by the powers that be.

The police force paraded majestically by in the streets of the district like Attila's horse spreading devastation on the face of the earth. Yes, law and order were re-established.

Among the numerous wounded we find Benito Alonso, one of our school companions who, while coming to school with his small books under his arm, was pierced by a bullet crazily shot by one of the government agents.

Benito Alonso is gravely wounded. We wish him a quick recovery.

The above was written by a 16-year-old member of the paper's staff. He grew up to be the President of the powerful Puerto Rican Confederation of Labor.

Reading that news story from the yellowish columns of *Adelante* now, I grant you it sounds too pompous and rhetorical. But it has a fire and truth in its lines.

Nothing in those schoolrooms of old Barracones has taught me as much as that encounter between the workers and the police that eventful day.

5. Stowaway

I still remember the name of the boat—S.S. Carolina. An old ship painted in funeral black around the hull and in hospital white from the deck up. Everything was planned with one of the crew. I just walked up the narrow wooden ladder of thin timber rungs far apart. This ladder connected the dock with the ships.

I think I don't have to explain that I did not carry a valise or other bundles with me. Just myself.

The sailor at the top of the ladder must have thought that I was one of those kids always going up and down with messages to the passengers. I was sixteen years old. As soon as I was inside the S. S. Carolina the friend on the crew installed me uncomfortably inside one of the linen closets, banging the door practically right on my nose. Time passed. The minutes seemed like hours. The hours felt like days. At last I heard the clanking of chains as the anchor was hoisted. After a little while I listened to the metallic noise of the propellers as they started their enormous metal four leaf clovers circling in the waters of San Juan Bay.

The third shrill whistle of the ship gave me the sign that we were finally getting away from the dock. I imagined from my hiding place in the linen closet that the S. S. Carolina was now on its course pointing its prow toward the entrance under the watchful eye of Morro Castle. In my mind I could see that the Door of San Juan, centuries old with its gate surrounded by old granite blocks that had grown indefinite in color, would now be looking at the ship. This very door had also seen the wooden vessels of Ponce de Leon, one of Puerto Rico's first Governors, passing by and the powerful galleons of pirates like Drake, Morgan and Cumberland, about whom I so fondly read in my childhood. And now, after a few more brief moments, I would be able to see none of San Juan's walls and Puerto Rico's palm decorated shores even if I were on deck.

As it had to happen, somebody came for fresh new linen eventually. They found me there together with the linen they came to get. I was brought to the Captain. After a scene mixed with ire and sermonizing on his part, I was placed in the "merciful" hands of the chief steward who passed me over to the chef in charge of the kitchen.

There I was introduced to the tallest mountain of pots, pans and cauldrons I had ever seen in my life. The general idea was that I was supposed to keep them shiny as a new Lincoln copper penny all through the voyage. I was also entrusted with the cleaning and washing of mounds of plates and cups of all shapes and sizes made out of cheap heavy porcelain. In an argument you could strike somebody with one of the heavy coffee cups and knock him cold. There was no regard for extra fine cleaning and washing. No taking your time in the precise and artistic handling of plates, saucers and other dishes. It seemed to me as if they had assigned a quota on each porcelain item that they could break during the voyage and they were very much afraid that they would not do enough breaking to fulfill and surpass their stated quotas.

It was simply a question of quantity against quality in dish washing. You just could not stop to see if the image of your sweaty, dirty face would truly be reflected in the plate that you just cleaned, washed and shined, for the chef might think that you were just stalling for time or perhaps just trying to get one minute's rest. And that was unthinkable. And the water in which you washed those dishes! We should not really call it water. We should rather call it steam converted into water. When you dipped your hands and forearms into it, you felt for a moment as if they were being melted into nothingness. It took me a few days to get my skin accustomed to the pain produced by the steam they called warm water, used on ships to wash dishes in those days.

Besides these kitchen chores, the other tasks of an average stowaway was to mop the floors, shine brass,—and do anything that anybody aboard ship thought he might place upon your shoulders to lighten his particular daily responsibilities. And don't you dare protest!

Good thing that I had a little experience at serving on tables in Puerto Rico! Little by little the steward of the second class dining room took notice of the fact, and I graduated into the class of an overworked bus boy who ran from table to table bringing back to the kitchen each time two armfuls of empty china.

Thus passed the days and nights traveling under strict war regulations, darkness during the night—for the United States was at war with Germany. During the day, I was shining dishes and pans or collecting china from the tables. During the night I went to bed too tired even to be able to dream about them.

One day I heard a voice hollering: "Sandy Hook, Sandy Hook!" I asked, "What is Sandy Hook?" "Sandy Hook is the name of one place in the land," somebody answered. None of Columbus' companions could have been happier than I at hearing that word LAND!

The steward had been watching the way I worked in the kitchen and dining room. One day he came to me. "How would you like to stay and work on this ship? Thirty dollars a month, room and board. One day off when we come to port." I did not answer him one way or the other. I just told him that I would think it over.

As the ship dropped anchor alongside a Brooklyn dock, and a plank connecting dock and ship was securely fastened in its place, I went ashore as unobtrusively as I had come into the boat in San Juan Bay in Puerto Rico. I never came back to accept the steward's offer to remain on the ship.

Good thing that I didn't, for a few trips later the S. S. Carolina was sent to the bottom of the Caribbean by a German submarine.

6. Easy Job, Good Wages

This happened early in 1919. We were both out of work, my brother and I. He got up earlier to look for a job. When I woke up, he was already gone. So I dressed, went out and bought a copy of the *New York World* and turned its pages until I got to the "Help Wanted Unskilled" section of the paper. After much reading and re-reading the same columns, my attention was held by a small advertisement. It read: "Easy job. Good wages. No experience necessary." This was followed by a number and street on the west side of lower Manhattan. It sounded like the job I was looking for. Easy job. Good wages. Those four words revolved in my brain as I was travelling toward the address indicated in the advertisement. Easy job. Good wages. Easy job. Good wages. Easy . . .

The place consisted of a small front office and a large loft on the floor of which I noticed a series of large galvanized tubs half filled with water out of which I noticed protruding the necks of many bottles of various sizes and shapes. Around these tubs there were a number of workers, male and female, sitting on small wooden benches. All had their hands in the water of the tub, the left hand holding a bottle and with the thumb nail of the right hand scratching the labels.

The foreman found a vacant stool for me around one of the tubs of water. I asked why a penknife or a small safety razor could not be used instead of the thumb nail to take off the old labels from the bottles. I was expertly informed that knives or razors would scratch the glass thus depreciating the value of the bottles when they were to be sold.

I sat down and started to use my thumb nail on one bottle. The water had somewhat softened the transparent mucilage used to attach the label to the bottle. But the softening did not work out uniformly somehow. There were always pieces of label that for some obscure reason remained affixed to the bottles. It was on those pieces of labels tenaciously fastened to the bottles that my right hand thumb nail had to work overtime. As the minutes passed I noticed that the coldness of the water started to pass from my hand to my body giving me intermittent body shivers that I tried to conceal with the greatest of effort from those sitting beside me. My hands became deadly clean and tiny little wrinkles started to show especially at the tip of my fingers. Sometimes I stopped a few seconds from scratching the bottles, to open and close my fists in rapid movements in order to bring blood to my hands. But almost as soon as I placed them in the water they became deathly pale again.

But these were minor details compared with what was happening to the thumb of my right hand. From a delicate, boyish thumb, it was growing by the minute into a full blown tomato colored finger. It was the only part of my right hand remaining blood red. I started to look at the workers' thumbs. I noticed that these particular fingers on their right hands were unusually developed with a thick layer of corn-like surface at the top of their right thumb. The nails on their thumbs looked coarser and smaller than on the other fingers—thumb and nail having become one and the same thing—a primitive unnatural human instrument especially developed to detach hard pieces of labels from wet bottles immersed in galvanized tubs.

After a couple of hours I had a feeling that my thumb nail was going to leave my finger and jump into the cold water in the tub. A numb pain imperceptibly began to be felt coming from my right thumb. Then I began to feel such pain as if coming from a finger bigger than all of my body.

After three hours of this I decided to quit fast. I told the foreman so, showing him my swollen finger. He figured I had earned 69 cents at 23 cents an hour.

Early in the evening I met my brother in our furnished room. We started to exchange experiences of our job hunting for the day. "You know what?" my brother started, "early in the morning I went to work where they take labels off old bottles—with your right hand thumb nail . . . Somewhere on the West Side of Lower Manhattan. I only stayed a couple of hours. 'Easy job . . . Good wages' . . . they said. The person who wrote that ad must have had a great sense of humor." And we both had a hearty laugh that evening when I told my brother that I also went to work at that same place later in the day.

Now when I see ads reading, "Easy job. Good wages," I just smile an ancient, tired, knowing smile.

7.   Two Men With But One Pair of Pants

The other evening my wife, Concha, was asking me: "Why don't you write a sketch about the man who, though he was seeing you for the first time in his life, placed a ten dollar bill in your hand when you told him you were out of work. Then he said you could pay him back some time in the future." After a pause my wife continued: "I remember that Sunday, soon after we were married, that you told me: 'Today we are going to pay ten dollars to a man.'"

"I remember very well," I answered. "I was only able to pay him back because at the time I insisted that he give me his address. And he was still living in the same place. He was a worker from Venezuela. A baker by trade."

"So why didn't you write a sketch about him?" my wife insisted.

"Because there are things that happen to you in life and if you write about them, nobody will believe you."

"I suppose that's why some people say that truth is stranger than fiction," Concha added a little philosophically.

"Take for instance the time my brother was working nights as a porter in the subway from seven until four in the morning. At the same time I was working days somewhere in Hoboken. It must have been around 1918."

My wife did not say a word because she knew that I was to start one of those episodes of my youth, of which she knew very little.

My brother's job was to keep the long, cold desolate platforms of a subway station nicely clean, to wash the toilets and see that the drunks didn't spoil his artistic brooming. Among his other multiple little tasks he had to collect all the newspapers and press them into bales that were stacked at the end of the station. For this he got about sixteen dollars a week for working from seven to four in the morning.

While he worked nights I worked days. So we hardly talked to each other during the week.

But one thing we did every evening as I came in was for me to hand him my working pants. He put them on, the pants still warm with the heat of my body. Then he said "Hasta manana" and left. When he came at 4:30 or 5 in the morning I was fast asleep. At seven in the morning I took back my working pants, put them on, without disturbing his sleep and off to work I went until the evening. When I came in at about six he took my—our—pants back.

The question might be asked: "And what did you do when both of you would go out say—on Sunday?" To that I would answer that we had our Sunday suits. I could not call them Sunday best, because "best" implies that there were other suits in our wardrobe with which a comparison of "good," "better" and "best" could be made. But we had no other suits. Just two. His and mine. And a pair of working pants for the both of us. Then again we could not call our suits "Sunday best," because our two Sunday suits had seen their best days already many, many, years ago. They were two blue serge suits whose seat-shine seemed to have permanently permeated the other parts of the cloth. Those were the two invaluable suits that were worn when we were not working.

But the fact remained that we only had one pair of working pants between the two of us. And that was a fact for months, until the day when we were not too tired after one of us came from work, to go out and buy one pair of pants. By that I really mean, until we could spare the few dollars—the cost of a pair of good working pants—without disturbing the very delicate balance between what we earned and what we had to spend on room, food, and other incidentals.

"Life is indeed stranger than fiction." Concha repeated, trying to give conviction with her voice to that oft repeated saying.

8. On The Docks It Was Cold

I open this old black tin box once every five or six years. There I keep things that have made a mark or change in my life. Here is the red membership card they gave me when I joined the Socialist Party of the United States at its Tompkins Park Branch in Brooklyn around the year 1923. Here is the first photograph Concha gave me from a Kodak box camera . . . thin and delicate like a soul with a skirt and a blouse on. And here is that old working badge from the yards of the Lackawanna Railroad. About forty years ago I swore I would never change it for the money that was owed me upon its presentation for payment. For this badge reminded me of my experiences as a dock and train-yard worker.

I started on what were in those days called the Hamburg American Line docks in Hoboken. They were the long streamlined docks taken over from the Germans by the United States government during the first World War. The dockworkers seemed to me to be all "six-footers." The ones who were visibly smaller were built like beer barrels to which legs of football players had been attached by nature.

When Mr. Clark, the big tall Negro foreman with the gangling walk, told me: "You're on," I did not believe it. As he kept on talking, it started to make sense. "You are young, small and light in weight. We need somebody like you. Somebody to go up on top of the piled-up sacks and release the 'knot' on top. There are many chores on the docks that could be handled better by light men. We will teach you the ropes." As time went on, I learned Mr. Clark's "ropes" and a few other tricks of the trade from the workers which proved to me in practice what my uncle Marcelo liked to say very often: "Mas vale mana que fuerza." "It is better to have skill than strength."

When the transport Batterland came in from France during

30

the first World War, it carried back thousands of canned food boxes, camp tents and boxes of small tent pegs. Those boxes were piled up in stacks of twos and fours that extended high up toward the dock's ceiling. At the top of each stack, two or four boxes were placed in such positions as to "tie" the stack together. When we received the order to place boxes in one of the transport ships, somebody had to go up to the top of each of those piles using nimble feet and a fine sense of balance, sharp quick reflexes and sharp eyes. They had to untie these by seeing that the boxes on top came into the same position as the others. With a sure, but swift push with one foot, while balancing on the other side of the stack with the other foot, you could see from the top how boxes came down to the dock floor. It was similar to those circus acrobats who, after standing on each other's shoulders for a moment decide to come down together from their human tower into the circus arena . . . Mr. Clark took me into his gang and told me how to do these simple things. Simple, after you knew how. Simple if you were young, a little carefree and adventurous.

I liked Mr. Clark. We all liked him and respected him very much. This respect and liking were the result of the knowledge he had about wharves, docks and dockwork in general. A knowledge that he demonstrated time and again. I never knew Mr. Clark's name. I think very few people knew it. But we all knew that he was born in Panama of Jamaican parents. Perhaps his father was one of those workers from Jamaica and the other English-speaking West Indies islands, who went to Panama at the beginning of the century to give their youth and blood in the building of the Panama Canal. Mr. Clark spoke fluently in many languages —Spanish, French, English—just as the descendants of West Indians frequently do and so too do many of the inhabitants of the islands. He knew how to load a ship better than anybody else . . . What should be loaded first, and what should go after. And what is more important, how to secure and place everything in the ship's bottom, so that no matter what the whims of the waves and storms, the cargo would stay right where Mr. Clark told us to place it.

Mr. Clark taught me everything of the art and science of using the hook . . . that very valuable all-purpose instrument of the dockworker. After you knew what to do and how to do it, you felt at home on a dock. Then you sort of sensed that Mr. Clark was there somewhere watching every move you made. He told us how to watch and safeguard each other's life and limb. Our gang was like a well-integrated team in which everybody participated in every move and decision and by which you were benefiting every hour as a result of the long work experience of everybody else.

It was in a certain way very funny. Everybody was Joe and Jack and Pedro and Tony but we only had one mister . . . that was Mr. Clark

The only thing that bothered me from the beginning was the coldness of the docks. It was so cold during the winter that, if you spat on the floor, the spit almost instantly converted itself into a round greyish spot of ice.

Besides the heavy working shoes that we all wore, we had gotten ourselves some burlap sacks that we used to tie around our heavy shoes and legs making us walk in a zig-zag fashion like old bears ready for their final icy resting place. Most of us wore heavy undergarments which covered us from the shoulders down to our ankles. Over them we wore a heavy woolen shirt, and an old vest, muffler, coat and overcoat with a rope around the waist. We used to hang the hook from there when we were not using it. With all this you had to be jumping constantly from one foot to the other, keeping in motion doing something or other in order to generate heat for your cold body. The intermittent run to the dock lavatories was mostly to hog a place in front of the plumber's pipes attached to the walls and used as steam heat radiators. After a moment there, you went back to the docks and believe it or not, you felt the cold more.

The war finished, our gang dispersed around the docks of the New York-New Jersey waterfronts. For a time, I could not find any work. Finally I found work . . . trucking . . . at what they called the fruit docks at the foot of Chambers Street on the Hudson River side. Times were very bad. It was what they called the period of readjustment. You had to take any kind of work to keep body and soul together. Some forty years ago I worked on those fruit docks from 11:30 at night to eight o'clock in the morning at $2.75 for an 8-hour day . . . that is night. And all the apples and pears that you could disentangle from the fragile fruit boxes. We got half an hour for "lunch" at three-thirty in the morning. The only trouble with the fruit docks was that they were colder than the Hamburg American docks in Hoboken. It was real cold at the fruit docks. It seemed to me that the owner kept them that way, with hardly any steam in the men's lavatory so that you would not have the tendency to sit overlong in the toilet and so that you would have to be moving and on the go during the whole time you were working.

Another bad feature of the fruit docks during those years was that the hand trucks were the old fashioned ones with the two big wheels on the outside, heavy and burdensome to manage. But the worst part of the fruit docks was that after you came back from "lunch," at four in the morning, the light fruit boxes of pears, apples and peaches converted themselves as if by magic into the heavy little nail barrels that you see beside the counter of the old-fashioned hardware stores and other similar "light" articles to tickle your back as you trucked along during the night over the bumpy, cold pavement. You were supposed to carry three of those stout little nail barrels in your hand truck each time it was loaded for you.

One morning, as I was coming from work on the fruit dock, I met one of the workers in Mr. Clark's old gang. He told me that they were looking for me as our old gang was getting together to work for the Lackawanna Railroad next day. He told me where they were to meet. I did not go back to work on the fruit docks any more. I went with Mr. Clark to work on the Lackawanna Railroad.

Your work did not actually start until you were placed on one of the numerous trunk trains, river barges or storage houses that Lackawanna had on both sides of the river. Some days it took half an hour walking in the snow, hail and cold weather before a call from the general office could tell us where our gang was most needed. The last day I worked there we were assigned to unload train wagons of coffee bags onto barges on the river below. The train wagons and the barges were connected by heavy gangplanks on which you almost had to fly to get to the barge while handling your handtruck with two heavy bags of coffee. While almost flying with the handtruck preceding you, one man in front of you, one on your heels, there were about half-a-dozen truckers on the barge trying to get away from where they figured you would land with your truck and coffee bags, while others were already moving themselves away in the train wagon on another less steep gangplank. As you reached the floor of the barge you had to maneuver your hand truck in between the two men who were ready to take the coffee bags off your truck and stack them up with others on the barge. You had about a minute to complete the operation unless you wanted to get run over, hand truck and all, by the men who were coming down the gangplank after you.

One of the times I was coming down the plank, it seemed that I gained too much speed with the result that the hand truck reeled down on just its left wheel. The two bags on my hand truck were perilously inclined to one side. It seemed as if any minute they were going to leave my truck to be gobbled up in the icy, cold waters of the river down below. I thought and acted fast. I moved the whole left part of my body to the right while pressing down the truck with my right hand and arm to the floor of the gangplank for a few seconds. While doing this it seemed that a counterforce inclined my body and truck handles way out into the left and off the gangplank floor. While I was trying to place myself into position to continue, I found myself in the air and entirely off the gangplank for a few seconds. My eyes kept contemplating the murky cold water of the river through the two handles of the hand truck. Those were the longest few seconds I had experienced in my life. As I reached the surface of the barge safely with my two precious bags of coffee intact, I waited until the two workers took them off my truck I ran the empty truck up the other gangplank into the train wagon and instead of taking my turn on line to return to the barge I ran my truck into a corner. Without a word to anybody, I just left the Lackawanna yards without cashing in my badge.

And there is the badge looking at me from the bottom of my old tin box. After almost forty years its shining red and silver is fresh and brilliant as the very day Mr. Clark handed it to me that cold winter morning, saying: "You are on." There is the badge beside my old 1923 membership card in the Socialist Party, and the first picture of Concha—my wife—looking thin and delicate, like a soul with a skirt and blouse on. Anybody else who sees the badge will say: "Just another badge."

But to me it is not "Just another badge." To me it represents the millions of men and women on the seas and in the fields, in the mines and in the foundries, in the factories and on the docks who risk and lose their lives as their fathers' fathers have been doing for hundreds of years before them, every day doing thousands of dangerous tasks.

I would not say it will happen tomorrow. But one day in these United States the workers will ask themselves collectively: "For whom all this toil?" "For what?" And their collective answer will be heard around the world.

9. I Heard A Man Crying

Around 1918 I was living in a rooming house on Atlantic Avenue in Brooklyn. I was working then as a scaler. Long distances, long hours and the dirtiest kind of work you could imagine.

As the ships came in, a scaling crew moved in to clean the ship from top to bottom. Cleaning was done especially at the bottom, underneath the machine room, and inside and around the furnaces.

If the ship was an oil tanker, you had to go down to the bottom of that tank ship after the oil was pumped off and collect the oil that the pump was unable to swallow, with a small tin shovel and a pail. The pail was placed on a hook at the end of a rope and hoisted up by those working on deck. Pay was better "down below" than on deck, so I always chose to work inside the tanker. As the job was about finished we were supposed to "paint" the inside of the oil tank with Portland cement by just throwing cement at the inside walls of the oil-moist tank. Imagine twenty or twenty-five men throwing cement at the oily walls of an enclosed tank!

When we came out, our faces, eyes, brows and hair looked old and gray. We looked like the grandfathers of our own selves. Some winters when the snow and ice covered the river solidly, the temperature down below at the bottom of the oil tank was below zero. Good thing that we were given rubber boots which fastened at the top of our thighs and rubber pants, jackets and hats that made us look like old seafarers.

Everywhere we went at the bottom of that tank, we were followed by a long electrical wire at the end of which there were three or four electric bulbs protected from breakage by a wire net. Sometimes when we gave the order to hoist the pail filled with oil and we kept looking up at that hole through which a ray of sun kept mocking at us down below, the edge of the pail might abruptly hit the edge of the hole way up there and a splash of ice cold oil would come spattering down and smear your face and neck. Sometimes the oil used to run down your back until it reached the very tip of your spine . . . and more. So, no matter how you scrubbed yourself, some of the oil always remained all over your body from your head to your toes. When I took the old crosstown trolley car with its spongy yellow straw seats and sat in one of them on my way home, I usually left a mark of black moist oil like a great heart parted right down the middle.

It was way into the evening when I came in from my scaling job, I was very tired. The room was very cold, I chose to get into bed with all my clothes on instead of going through the task of starting a fire in the dead coal stove in the middle of the room. (Why is it so difficult for tropical people to start a fire in a hard coal stove?)

As if coming from way out in space through the cracks in my window and from the crevices dividing the door and the floor I heard a very low moaning sound. It went up and down like a wave. Then there was silence for a minute or two and then it started all over again in a repressed way as if the person from whom the crying, moaning sound came did not want to be heard by anybody. Then as if the pain or emotion could not be held back anymore a piercing cry full of self-pity and desperation came distinctly to my ears. At last I could trace clearly from whence it came. It was from another room on the same floor. I knocked at the door of the room. After a short pause, the door was opened by a man who then turned and sat himself on a narrow bed which filled the room.

He covered his face with his hands and then let his crying run fully. I could see that the man was robust, built strong as a bull. He was possibly accustomed to heavy work out of doors. It was sad, yes, tragic, to listen to such a specimen of man crying. So clumsily and innocently strong was he.

In between the minutes that he could control his emotions and his natural shyness, he told me of missing a boat where he was working as a coal passer. The boat belonged to a Spanish shipping company. He himself was Spanish. A story of the ignorance of the language, of fear of the immigration laws, of shyness and of pride, not to beg, not to ask for anything, followed.

The man had not eaten since . . . he didn't remember how many days. He was actually starving, gradually dying of hunger.

Have you ever heard a man crying? A young strong man crying? Crying of hunger in the midst of what is supposed to be the greatest and richest city in the world? It is the saddest, most tragic sight you could ever imagine.

At that hour we left the rooming house and went to the nearest restaurant. He ate as if he had never eaten before in his life.

Next day I took him to an old iron junk yard in which they were asking for young strong men. The job was to break old iron parts of machinery with a sledge hammer. My new Spanish friend wielded the big sledge hammer with the gracefulness and ease of a young girl skipping a thin rope on the sidewalk.

For the first few days I managed to bring him to his place of work. Then he would wait for me in the evening at the wide door of the junk yard until he learned how to take the trolley car that would take him to and from the rooming house where we were living.

I moved. I don't remember the last time I saw that burly, strong young Spaniard.

But I will never forget as long as I live, his deep anguished crying of hunger that night—long, long ago.

10. Kipling And I

        Sometimes I pass Debevoise Place at the corner of Willoughby Street . . . I look at the old wooden house, gray and ancient, the house where I used to live some forty years ago . . .

My room was on the second floor at the corner. On hot summer nights I would sit at the window reading by the electric light from the street lamp which was almost at a level with the window sill.

It was nice to come home late during the winter, look for some scrap of old newspaper, some bits of wood and a few chunks of coal and start a sparkling fire in the chunky fourlegged coal stove. I would be rewarded with an intimate warmth as little by little the pigmy stove became alive puffing out its sides, hot and red, like the crimson cheeks of a Santa Claus.

My few books were in a soap box nailed to the wall. But my most prized possession in those days was a poem I had bought in a five and ten cent store on Fulton Street. (I wonder what has become of these poems, maxims and sayings of wise men that they used to sell at the five and ten cent stores?) The poem was printed on gold paper and mounted in a gilded frame ready to be hung in a conspicuous place in the house. I bought one of those fancy silken picture cords finishing in a rosette to match the color of the frame.

I was seventeen. This poem to me then seemed to summarize the wisdom of all the sages that ever lived in one poetical nutshell. It was what I was looking for, something to guide myself by, a way of life, a compendium of the wise, the true and the beautiful. All I had to do was to live according to the counsel of the poem and follow its instructions and I would be a perfect man—the useful, the good, the true human being. I was very happy that day, forty years ago.

The poem had to have the most prominent place in the room.

Where could I hang it? I decided that the best place for the poem was on the wall right by the entrance to the room. No one coming in and out would miss it. Perhaps someone would be interested enough to read it and drink the profound waters of its message . . .

Every morning as I prepared to leave, I stood in front of the poem and read it over and over again, sometimes half a dozen times. I let the sonorous music of the verse carry me away. I brought with me a handwritten copy as I stepped out every morning looking for work, repeating verses and stanzas from memory until the whole poem came to be part of me. Other days my lips kept repeating a single verse of the poem at intervals throughout the day.

In the subways I loved to compete with the shrill noises of the many wheels below by chanting the lines of the poem. People stared at me moving my lips as though I were in a trance. I looked back with pity. They were not so fortunate as I who had as a guide to direct my life a great poem to make me wise, useful and happy.

And I chanted:

> *If you can keep your head when all about you*
> *Are losing theirs and blaming it on you . . .*
>
> *If you can wait and not be tired by waiting*
> *Or being hated don't give way to hating . . .*
>
> *If you can make one heap of all your winnings*
> *And risk it on a turn of pitch and toss . . .*
> *And lose and start again at your beginnings . . .*

"If," by Kipling, was the poem. At seventeen, my evening prayer and my first morning thought. I repeated it every day with the resolution to live up to the very last line of that poem.

I would visit the government employment office on Jay Street. The conversations among the Puerto Ricans on the large wooden benches in the employment office were always on the same subject.

How to find a decent place to live. How they would not rent to Negroes or Puerto Ricans. How Negroes and Puerto Ricans were given the pink slips first at work.

From the employment office I would call door to door at the piers, factories and storage houses in the streets under the Brooklyn and Manhattan Bridges. "Sorry, nothing today." It seemed to me that that "today" was a continuation and combination of all the yesterdays, todays and tomorrows.

From the factories I would go to the restaurants looking for a job as a porter or dishwasher. At least I would eat and be warm in a kitchen.

"Sorry" . . . "Sorry" . . .

Sometimes I was hired at ten dollars a week, ten hours a day including Sundays and holidays. One day off during the week. My work was that of three men: dishwasher, porter, busboy. And to clear the sidewalk of snow and slush "when you have nothing else to do." I was to be appropriately humble and grateful not only to the owner but to everybody else in the place.

If I rebelled at insults or at a pointed innuendo or just the inhuman amount of work, I was unceremoniously thrown out and told to come "next week for your pay." "Next Week" meant weeks of calling for the paltry dollars owed me. The owners relished this "next week."

I clung to my poem as to a faith. Like a potent amulet, my precious poem was clenched in the fist of my right hand inside my second hand overcoat. Again and again I declaimed aloud a few precious lines when discouragement and disillusionment threatened to overwhelm me.

If you can force your heart and nerve and sinew
To serve your turn long after you are gone . . .

The weeks of unemployment and hard knocks turned into months. I continued to find two or three days of work here and there. And I continued to be thrown out when I rebelled at the ill treatment, overwork and insults. I kept pounding the streets looking for a place where they would treat me half decently, where my devotion to work and faith in Kipling's poem would be appreciated. I remember the worn out shoes I bought in a second-hand store on Myrtle Avenue at the corner of Adams Street. The round holes in the soles that I tried to cover with pieces of carton were no match for the frigid knives of the unrelenting snow.

One night I returned late after a long day of looking for work. I was hungry. My room was dark and cold. I wanted to warm my numb body. I lit a match and began looking for some scraps of wood and a piece of paper to start a fire. I searched all over the floor. No wood, no paper. As I stood up, the glimmering flicker of the dying match was reflected in the glass surface of the framed poem. I unhooked the poem from the wall. I reflected for a minute, a minute that felt like an eternity. I took the frame apart, placing the square glass upon the small table. I tore the gold paper on which the poem was printed, threw its pieces inside the stove and placing the small bits of wood from the frame on top of the paper I lit it adding soft and hard coal as the fire began to gain strength and brightness.

I watched how the lines of the poem withered into ashes inside the small stove.

11. How To Rent An Apartment Without Money

A good way to find out if a Puerto Rican has been in New York over forty years is by asking him if he knew Markofsky. Markofsky had a coat and suit store somewhere on Second Avenue near 106th Street. The store looked like a tunnel with racks of suits and coats dangling from the walls. This tunnel of suits and coats had a little space in the back with a desk from which Markofsky waded out to greet you as you came in.

Old man Markofsky was quite a guy among the Puerto Ricans of those days. He was your clothier on the long, long instalment plan. His name and his store was even mentioned in one of the most popular dance pieces of those days.

Markofsky was small, a little over five feet. His pace was deliberate, his steps were short. He walked a little bent to the front. He had a sort of dignity and confidence in his walk. His face always wore a sad smile over which he superimposed a cigar. If you observed him well, he seemed like a biblical patriarch who liked to be eternally smoking a cigar.

As soon as anybody came from Puerto Rico—especially during the winter—you would take him to Markofsky. Markofsky would take care of outfitting him with a winter suit and a heavy coat to repel the winter cold. Then the newcomer was set to go out and look for a job. All you had to do was to put two dollars on top of Markofsky's old desk and you walked out with an overcoat. Your credit would be good if you came with two dollars every week for a certain number of weeks. If you kept it up steadily and did not miss any weekly payments, I know you could even "touch" Markofsky sometimes for a five "until Saturday," when you received that urgent letter from Puerto Rico asking for a little extra money that week for some emergency.

My brother and I had reached the "touching" stage with old benign Markofsky.

We had to have an apartment. Our family was coming from Puerto Rico and we did not even have the money to pay the first month's rent or to buy a bed or a couch, to say nothing of tables and chairs. So we went to Markofsky. Instead of asking for a five "until Saturday," we asked to see the new suits that were just coming in. The jackets of the suits had belts with very wide shiny buckles. The suits looked very sporty and fashionable and they cost quite a bit of money.

The suits fitted in perfectly with our plans. The more they cost, the better. Markofsky gave us two identical suits with the usual small down payment.

From the store we went directly to a pawn shop a few blocks away. We pawned the two suits that we just bought. With the money we got from the pawn shop we paid the first month's rent on an apartment on 143rd Street between Lenox and Seventh. In those days the few Puerto Ricans around lived in the heart of the Negro neighborhood together with the Negro people in the same buildings; many times as roomers in their homes. Rents were not so high thirty-five years ago.

That very afternoon we got the keys to the apartment—a "railroad" flat. My brother and I felt great.

Night came. We went to the home where we were rooming. Took our two suitcases, said goodbye and thanks and went to our long empty apartment. My brother went into the parlor, laid himself on the floor and with his suitcase as his pillow went to sleep as if he were in the Waldorf Astoria. I did likewise, lying down beside him with my own suitcase as my pillow. After a few minutes we were both sound asleep. Many a night we had to sleep like that.

The family came: mother, father, sisters, brothers, cousins, and just friends who, because of living with us so many years, had become part of the family. An old Puerto Rican custom. Many times we asked mother about someone who had been living with us for years. "In what way is Jose related to us?" And my mother, after a lot of genealogical hemming and hawing in which the more she explained the more she got involved and confused, would end with a desperate whimsical gesture: "He is just part of the family." And there it ended.

We moved to Brooklyn. Every year either my brother or myself went over to the pawn shop in New York and renewed the tickets for the suits, paying the interest and letting it ride.

One year we were in the chips and instead of renewing the pawn shop tickets we actually took out the two suits. I was saying to myself: "Now I have a new suit with which I can go out to dance the Charleston this coming Saturday night."

But we had not counted on one thing—time. When my brother and I unpacked the "new" suits that we had hardly seen, the color was something between one shade and another, but nothing definite. The lack of air in the closeness of the pawn shop vaults had played havoc with the material and the texture. After we took off the multiple tickets sewed to the pants and jackets, we started for the first time to thoroughly examine the cut and style of the two suits and compare them with what the young sports were wearing those days. The buckles and belts on the jackets looked like something out of a pageant of the medieval ages. When we finally put the suits on and looked at ourselves in the mirror we certainly felt as if we were seeing ourselves in one of those distorted freak mirrors in which you laugh at your own figure when you go to Coney Island.

We had certainly changed in a few years. We were fatter and even taller. The pants were too short. The coat sleeves reached just below the elbows. In short, we looked too ridiculous for words. We laughed very loudly at ourselves until tears came out of our eyes.

We should cry all right. That cheap first apartment we rented in New York came to be one for which we actually paid the highest first month's rent in our lives.

12. The Day My Father Got Lost

I was working in a factory with my brother in Brooklyn during the First World War. The shop manufactured woolen leggings and caps for the army. In front of the place where we worked, on the other side of the street, there was a big department store. My brother and I brought our mother, our father and the rest of the family from Puerto Rico. We were living in a railroad apartment on 143rd Street near Lenox Avenue. One day we thought that if we brought our father with us to the place where we worked in Brooklyn, perhaps we might be able to find a job for him.

The three of us went into the factory in the morning. We asked the foreman if there was something our father could do. The foreman told us there was nothing for him at the moment. "Keep on bringing him every day—somebody is liable to leave or not show up."

My brother and I started to work. My father sat somewhere out of the way. After we lunched he asked us if he could just take a walk and look around until our day's work was over and we could all go back home to Harlem.

Father did not know a word of English. Furthermore my good father was not too familiar with the first two of the three R's, even in Spanish. The third he just disregarded altogether. So to send him back home all by himself was out of the question. Before he started to walk around the factory neighborhood he looked at the things that attracted his attention. My father took a good look at all the objects that he could see in the department store window. He went as far as memorizing the color of the dresses the lady mannikins were wearing. He took the department store window and all that it contained as the sign where he had to return to after he got tired of whiling away time walking around the streets near the factory.

There were about one hundred men and women making woolen

leggings and caps where we were working. Every item was supposed to be thoroughly examined by government examiners. Nothing that was the least bit defective was to be sent to the boys in France. But the opposite was the customary thing to do. Rotten old woolen material was used in the manufacture of this indispensable woolen apparel for the soldiers in France. The government examiners okayed anything, stamping their seal of approval on all that was sent to the soldiers in the front line Why did the examiners do it? I will let you take just one guess. It seemed to my innocent young mind that on pay day the government examiners were happier than usual.

While father was leisurely promenading through the streets of Brooklyn, those in charge of the department store had chosen to change the display in that part of the window that my father had memorized in all its details. This was done without asking the consent of my father. Perhaps, out of elementary courtesy, they should have sent somebody to tell him they were changing the displays.

Tired of walking, father decided to come to his original place of departure: the department store window. This was the sign that would tell him that he was at the right spot. But, lo and behold! the display that he had memorized so thoroughly was changed.

He came to the store window. But he did not see any of the things he could have sworn he had seen there in the early afternoon. In a moment of confusion he decided that the store window he was seeing in the late afternoon was not the store window he had seen before he decided to take a little walk. He further decided in his mind that neither the store nor the street was the one in which his sons were working.

As my brother and I came out of the factory to go home, we looked around confident that we would find our father standing somewhere in front of the building waiting for us. We waited and then looked around some more on the streets nearest to the factory. No father in sight. Then we expanded the circle so to speak, and started looking in a wider area. No, we could not find father. We decided that perhaps it would be wise if I looked on some streets and avenues while my brother looked into some others. We agreed upon a certain time to come together at a predetermined corner we both knew well. This was done. After hours of looking around we got together at the agreed upon corner—without our father.

We decided to go home. We took the long subway ride from Brooklyn to 145th Street and Lenox Avenue subway station in Harlem. During the subway ride we were preparing ourselves for the rap we were sure going to take from the rest of the family when we told them that we lost our father in Brooklyn.

As we came in, there was a look of surprise on every face as we sank into a couple of chairs, tired and hungry, and informed the family gathered around us that our father was lost somewhere in the heart of Brooklyn. Strange to say, there were no questions asked. No excitement. No reproaches. A heavy silence served as a pall to conversation. Still there was an expression of mock surprise on everyone's face. All of a sudden we heard a voice from the farthest room in our railroad flat. "Hello, sons, I am safe and sound. The police brought me in. Good thing I had the address of this building on a piece of paper."

Then we had a good tired laugh while father told us all about his wandering in an unknown far away country called Brooklyn.

13. Hiawatha Into Spanish

The old *New York World* was a great paper. I bought it mainly for the Heywood Broun column "It Seems To Me," and for the pages and pages of Help Wanted Ads. I got many a "good" porter job through these Help Wanted pages of the *New York World*. Once, I also got myself a job as a translator from these same pages.

Those were the days of the silent films. A film agency somewhere in the Times Square area was asking for a person who could translate the explanatory material like "One Year Later," into Spanish, so that the films could be used in Latin America. Half a penny a word was to be paid. The translator was to work in his own home and all transactions were to be done through the mail. The agency gave a post office box number to which you were supposed to write.

I wrote. The agency mailed me the material to be translated for one short film. I returned the completed translation. Then they sent me a small check, and more work. It seems that they were satisfied.

Time passed. My old Oliver typewriting machine continued to grind translations of inspirational thoughts such as: "The morning after," "One week after," "Five years after." Sometimes a description or historical paragraph such as an introduction to a striking panorama or a scene helped to break the monotony of the hackneyed phrase and the routine short dialogue.

During the early twenties, the episode or chapter of a serial was a standard feature accompanying the main picture in a movie house. At the end of the episode the hero or more often the heroine was left hanging by two fingers from the edge of a cliff or surrounded by half a dozen lions in the middle of an African jungle. The idea was to excite enough curiosity for you to return next week to see what surely appeared, from all logical deduction, like certain death for the hero or heroine. But—what do you know! She or he was miraculously saved from a horrible ending by one of the thousand props that the director always had ready to extract from his shirt sleeve and the serial went on and on for months. Today, you can only see these serials chapter by chapter every week in the cheapest of the movie houses or on the most idiotic of the TV programs.

To me, these serials were a gold mine. I was the first to wish the hero eternal life—the longer the serials, the more money I could earn.

One morning I received a long poem that was supposed to be the life of a young American Indian. It was to be used in one of those nature pictures full of rushing rivers, whispering pine trees, bounding deer and flocks of birds suddenly rising out of the thick foliage frightened by the unexpected appearance of "man." The poem was long. The name of the poem was "Hiawatha" by Henry Wadsworth Longfellow. Well, at last I got something worth translating! For a few days I concentrated on making a comparative study of the English and Spanish meter, poetic accent, rhyme and rhythm, before I actually tackled the task of translating the poem itself. It was work. It was fun. Some additional explanation in prose helped in giving clarity and unity to the many natural scenes in the film. The poem itself was broken into sections and these were inserted among the panoramic sequences. When I finished the translation I felt I had done a good job of it.

Hiawatha was sent to the film agency. A few days later I received a complimentary letter with a check. The letter also invited me to come to the office on a certain date. I was being offered steady employment at the agency at a weekly salary.

I got up very early the day of the appointment. I took a great deal of time washing, dressing and combing my hair so that I would look my best. I wore my Sunday suit. The office took up about half an entire floor, way up in a tall building. I asked for the man who had signed the letter. Yes, he was in.

The minute I told him who I was and showed him the letter he himself had signed offering me steady work as a translator, he assumed a cold and impersonal attitude. He made it short and to the point. "Yes, I wrote that letter. I invited you to come to translate for us here at the office." And, pointing to the other side of the room he added "That was to be your desk and typewriter. But I thought you were white."

Then and there that day in the early twenties, I added one more episode to the maturing serial of my life.

14. Name In Latin

It was in the early nineteen twenties. The meeting was called for a Sunday afternoon. The man who extended the invitation for the meeting was a Latin-American printer-poet, self-exiled from his country. He had come to live in Greenwich Village.

We climbed four floors. It was a curious parlor that we entered on coming through the door of the apartment. It was a long spacious rectangle. On one side, close to the walls, there were two printer's stands. On these were various flat wooden boxes known as printer's fonts with squared off divisions in them. Each division contained metal samples of a single letter. The stands and the fonts seemed to be brand new, as also was a small foot press close to the other wall opposite the stands.

In amongst these printer's elementary needs, chairs, a couple of empty boxes and a small center table managed to bring to mind a reflection of a family parlor. As you peeked into the other rooms, you noticed what appeared to be second hand beds and couches. All the way back, at the other end of the railroad flat you could see a woman cooking in a small kitchen, surrounded by three kids who physically and vocally seemed to object very strongly to their mother's insistence on cooking at that time.

When I entered there were half a dozen others already sitting on the chairs and boxes in the parlor-printing room. Perhaps we should say printing room-parlor, as the furniture, type and press were newer and occupied more space than what might be properly called parlor furniture.

The printer-poet lost no time after two or three more people, who came after me, were seated. He got up and without more ado, gave us in detail the reason for calling the meeting. He gave us a summary of the history of the Latin American colony in the City. Then he enumerated the abuses and insults, discrimination and violation of our most elementary civil rights. He then finished with what in essence was the following:

"I am a very practical man, though as you all know I write poetry. In order to combat these abuses against the Latin Americans I came to the conclusion long ago that we needed a weekly publication . . . our voice in print. I also know that it takes money and work to print a weekly. So I bought these fonts and this foot press on the instalment plan. I am a printer. Shall I say more?"

There was quite a bit more to be said, especially if you looked at that project in the perspective acquired after over thirty-five years of multiple experiences. But in the early twenties, we were young and full of rosy ideas. Half a dozen type fonts and one small foot press. After all, Ben Franklin started the *Saturday Evening Post* with less.

"And now, proposals for a name" the printer-poet continued. "Come on, let us hear some proposals for a name, for our publication." These were some of the names proposed: they were all hard hitting names—"El Martillo" (The Hammer). "El Machete," (The Machete)—"El Despertar" (The Awakening). I proposed "Adelante" (Forward) which was the name of our monthly school publication in Puerto Rico, of which I had been the editor. All the names were discussed backward and forward. None met the approval of the majority.

"Well, I have a name to propose. I had not proposed any name up until now," the printer-poet said. And then he walked toward the foot press and placing his hand gently on top of the machine he said: "I propose that the publication which is going to be printed on this press be called *Vae Victis!*"

"Vae what?" all or most of us asked in unison. The poet-printer exile repeated slowly and sententiously: "*Vae Victis!*"

"What language is that?" "What does that mean?" The poet-printer was bombarded with questions from all corners. "Well, 'Vae victis,' in Spanish, means: 'Ay, de los vencidos!' In English, it means, 'Woe to the vanquished!' You understand now?"

A collective blank look into space by all those present was the answer he received. He felt that additional explanation was necessary. "Well it is like this—if we don't organize, if we don't raise our cry to the top of the highest skyscraper in New York, we are going to be crushed . . . we are going to be vanquished. Vae Victis! Woe

to the vanquished! We must not let this happen. We must protest.
We must talk, we must write; we must fight."

The printer-poet was very eloquent. To a number of "argu-
ments" that I could now see as only emotion wrapped in what
sounded like logical words, he added that the very newness of the
idea, the curiosity it would raise in the mind of the prospective
reader passing by a news stand would actually double its circulation over night. How could I vote in favor of naming a weekly for
Spansh-American readers in New York *Vae Victis!*? How foolish
it appears to me now! How wonderful and logical it sounded to me
then!

So *Vae Victis!* was the name selected. Without a subtitle in
English or Spanish on that all important cover page. We were that
confident. The format was slightly bigger than one of the modern
digest monthly publications that we have today. The small press
in the printer-poet's parlor would not allow anything larger than
that. While our printer-poet kept on for hours in front of the fonts
composing by hand, others were making up the small pages using
an old piece of marble from a discarded mantlepiece as the composing table. Still another was reading some proof of the pages
already made. Then we all pitched in collating pages and stapling
them. What a job!

At last the first issue of *Vae Victis!* was out! We divided ourselves according to the districts where the Spaniards, Puerto Ricans
and other Latin Americans used to live in those early years of the
nineteen-twenties.

So we had to write it, print it, proofread it, staple it, go around
and place it on the stands and come to collect the unsold copies
and return with the new number. That guy who kept rolling that
stone uphill to the top of the mountain a couple of thousand years
ago in Greece had nothing on us!

When I returned to the stands where I had left copies of *Vae
Victis!* all of them were returned to me. With very few exceptions, that was the experience of almost all the others who left
copies on other stands. I suppose the Greeks thought it was a publication for Italians, the Italians thought it was a magazine for the
Romanians, the Romanians thought it was a paper for the French

and so on to the last of all languages. Everybody thought our weekly was for somebody else's language, not their own. The only one who I could figure out would buy it, with its name in Latin, would be a stray young priest who happened to glance for a second at the glamor cover of the Police Gazette and wanted to release his soul from such a sin by buying a magazine he thought might be written in the language of the Catholic church.

Oh, how many foolish things you have to go through in life in order to gain just a bit of knowledge and experience! And, you want to know something? If a group like these young people of the early twenties came over and asked me today if I would be willing to repeat the experience, I sure would tell them yes.

The only thing is that I might put up a fight about putting the name in Latin. I might oppose them on that.

I had a copy of *Vae Victis!* somewhere. I don't know where I put it. I wish I could find it and keep it. For it will be a rare collector's item for that unborn researcher who will be writting the history of the Puerto Ricans in New York fifty years from now.

A few young fellows, way back at the beginning of the century started a paper, under far greater handicaps than we found with *Vae Victis!*

These young fellows did not have any printing press or fonts of their own. Many a time they did not have enough money to buy food for themselves.

Then they had to smuggle this small paper from the country where they printed it, into another country where frontier guards, the military and special secret police were all instructed to confiscate every copy of that little paper and throw those caught with it into jail.

Yes, these fellows in far away Europe certainly worked under many more difficulties than we encountered in bringing to life our *Vae Victis!*

One thing that they had to their advantage was the name of their paper, it was not in Latin. It was written in the language of the people for whom it was written. When the workers read it, the contents did not sound like Greek or Latin to them, for it was written for the people, in the language of the people, dealing with the problems of the people by a group of the greatest minds of that country. In fact the world is still discussing the articles and studies that these young men printed in this little paper and we have not yet heard the last word on the idea that they elaborated in the pages of their small publication.

This group of young "dreamers" and "idealists" as they would probably have been called by the "practical and sensible" persons of their day called their little paper: "The Spark," and by golly, they succeeded in starting a conflagration of thought and ideas with it all over the world.

That is why you should never say no, when they invite you to start the publication of a paper. Even if the name is in Latin. You never can tell what could come of it.

With all the thirty odd dailies, weeklies and monthlies that I have contributed to and worked with, in one way or another, I have gained a precious thing . . . experience.

That you have to earn yourself . . . by doing things that come out right, or by publishing a magazine with the name in Latin!

15. A Hero In The Junk Truck

How many times have we read boastful statements from high educational leaders in our big newspapers that while other countries ignore the history and culture of the United States, our educational system does instruct our children in the history and traditions of other countries.

As far as instruction in the most elementary knowledge of Latin America is concerned, we are forced to state that what our children receive is a hodgepodge of romantic generalities and chauvinistic declarations spread further and wider by Hollywood movies.

We do not have to emphasize that the people are not to blame.

Blame rests on those persons and reactionary forces that represent and defend the interests of finance capital in education.

Last summer my wife and I had an experience that could be presented as proof of our assertion.

We were passing by, on bus No. 37, my wife and I.

"Look, Jesus, look!" said my wife pointing excitedly to a junk truck in front of the building that was being torn down. A truck full of the accumulated debris of many years was parked with its rear to the sidewalk, littered with pieces of brick and powdered cement.

Atop the driver's cabin of the truck and protruding like a spangled banner, was a huge framed picture of a standing figure. Upon his breast was a double line of medals and decorations.

"Did you notice who the man was in that framed picture?" my wife asked insistently as the bus turned the corner of Adams and Fulton Street.

"Who," I answered absent mindedly.

"Bolivar," my wife shouted.

"Who did you say he was?" I inquired as if unduly awakened from a daze.

"Bolivar, Bolivar," my wife repeated excitedly and then she added, "and to think that he is being thrown out into a junk truck," she stammered in a breaking voice.

We got out of the bus in a hurry. Walked to where the truck was about to depart with the dead waste of fragments of a thousand things. The driver caught us staring at the picture.

"What do you want?" he shouted to us in a shrill voice above the noise of the acetylene torch and the electric hammers.

"You know who he is," I cried back pointing at the picture tied atop the cabin of the driver's truck like Joan of Arc tied to the flaming stake.

"I don't know and I don't care," the driver counter-blasted in a still higher pitch of voice. But I noticed that there was no enmity in the tone of his voice, though loud and ear-drum breaking.

"He is like George Washington to a score of Latin American countries. He is . . ."

"You want it?" he interrupted in a more softened voice.

"Of course!" my wife answered for both of us, just about jumping with glee.

As the man was unroping Bolivar from atop the truck cabin, the usual group of passersby started clustering around and encircling us—the truck driver, my wife, myself and Bolivar's painting standing erect and magnificent in the middle of us all.

"Who is he, who is he?" came the question of the inquiring voices from everywhere. The crowd was huddled on top of us, as football players ring themselves together bending from their trunks down when they are making a decision before the next play. "Who is he, I mean, the man in the picture?" they continued to ask.

Nobody knew. Nobody seemed to care really. The question was asked more out of curiosity than real interest. The ones over on the third line of the circle of people craned their necks over the ones on the second and first lines upping themselves on their tip toes in order to be able to take a passing glance at the picture. "He is not an American, is he?" someone inquired from the crowd.

My wife finally answered them with a tinge of pride in her voice. "He is Simon Bolivar, the liberator of Latin America."

Curiosity fulfilled, everybody was on his way again. Only my wife, myself and Bolivar remained.

Well, what to do next. It was obvious that the bus driver would not allow us in the bus with such a large framed painting going back home. Fortunately we have a very good American friend living in the Borough Hall neighborhood.

"Let us take him to John's place until we find a person with a car to take Bolivar to our home," I said. My wife agreed.

We opened the door of John's apartment.

"I see that you are coming with very distinguished company today:—'Bolivar,'" he said, simply and casually as if he had known it all his life.

John took some cleaning fluid and a soft rag and went over the whole frame in a loving and very tender manner.

We heard a knock at the door. In came a tall and very distinguished looking man dressed in black, a blend of Lincoln and Emerson in his personality. "He is a real representative of progressive America," John whispered to us. The Reverend spoke quietly and serenely. Looking at the picture he said just one word:

"Bolivar!"

And we all felt very happy.

16. Maceo*

Last night I received a telephone call from a very dear American friend. She said that she looked up Hostos, the great Puerto Rican thinker and educator of Latin America, in the *Encyclopedia Britannica*. She was very surprised to find that the name of Hostos was not listed in what is supposed to be the number one reference work of the English speaking world.

While I was listening to the latest radio news about Cuba—the magnificent students' stand, the open rebellion in the city of Matanzas and the gathering of the opposition forces against Wall Street Cuban dictator Batista all over the Cuban nation, I opened up one of the volumes of the great reference work and looked up Maceo, one of the most outstanding figures in Cuba's struggle for independence against Spanish imperialism. The name of Antonio Maceo—also was not listed in the *Encyclopedia Britannica*.

The fact that both Eugenio Maria de Hostos and Antonio Maceo, as well as many other Latin American patriots, writers, poets and thinkers are given substantial space in the other great European encyclopedias does not seem to disturb the compilers of the Britannica.

So we do not have to wonder much when the general public in the United States is so misinformed about what, for lack of a better short name, is called Latin America.

Maceo is a case in point. General Antonio Maceo y Grajales was a Cuban Negro born June 14, 1848 at Majaguabo, Santiago de Cuba.. He died in combat against the Spanish forces at Punta Brava on December 7, 1896. Maceo's father, Marcos, born in Venezuela, as well as General Maceo's eight brothers also gave their lives fighting for Cuban independence. Mariana was Maceo's mother. Her parents were born in Santo Domingo.

---

* This essay appeared in the *Daily Worker* on May 1, 1956, before the Cuban Revolution overthrew Batista on January 1, 1959.

To write about Maceo as a military genius who never knew what a military academy looked like, to record his hundreds of battles and encounters both in the 1868 and the 1895 Cuban struggles for independence, to set forth the elements of his practical strategy and tactics with which he outmaneuvered recognized European experts in these fields like General Martinez Campos and others, will take quite a bit of space.

All that space will permit us is to point out that Antonio Maceo was also the embodiment of Cuba's will toward national independence, a decided fighter against Negro slavery and for racial equality, a proven anti-imperialist. A thinker and preacher of Cuban unity. Maceo was all these because in his life as a laborer, as a teamster, as a guerilla fighter and as a soldier all through Cuba's land, he gathered within himself all the experiences and voices of the Cuban people. And in all his deeds and declarations we feel that it is not Maceo, the individual, giving expression to his own particular thoughts, but all that he did and said comes from the people. His eyes and ears and all his other senses were ever alert to the most subtle manifestations of the people's will.

Wherever Maceo went through his beloved Cuba or in his exiles in Jamaica, Honduras, Costa Rica, Panama, Peru or in New York, where he came to consult with Jose Marti and the Cuban Revolutionary Junta, Maceo was the continuous propagandist and fighter for Cuban indepedence.

Maceo's short, concrete and devastating answers to Cubans who thought in terms of annexing Cuba to the United States, or to those who wanted to surrender to the Spanish government's terms that were less than absolute and complete independence, are well known in Cuban patriotic literature.

Maceo said once: "As long as there is one injustice to be destroyed, the Cuban revolution has not finished."

In June 1948, the Cuban, Puerto Rican and other Spanish speaking members of the Hispanic colony of New York, celebrated the centenary of the birth of Antonio Maceo at Town Hall. It was indeed a night to be remembered. Great Cuban, Puerto Rican and other Spanish name orchestras, declaimers and entertainers offered their services absolutely free that cultural evening at Town

Hall. Senator Salvador Aguero, member of the Cuban Senate at that time and leader of the Cuban Socialist Popular Party, came especially from Havana to address this Town Hall gathering. How well do I remember the moment Senator Aguero started to detail the facts of American imperialism in Latin America and how the broadcasting company that was sending the program to the Spanish speaking countries informed us that the broadcasting apparatus suddenly went out of order!

As we are writing these lines, the Cuban people are going through one of their greatest struggles for real political, economic and social independence for their country. One day does not pass without news of another rebellious act against American imperialism in Cuba. The Cuban people know that there are still many "injustices to be destroyed" in Cuba. The Cuban storm is gathering momentum.

All the monies of Wall Street, and all the Pentagon, FBI and State Department advisers to American imperialism's majordomo Batista, will not be able to stop the Cuban people in their resolution to have true, progressive democracy in Cuba.

"When Cuba becomes independent I will ask for permission to struggle for the freedom of Puerto Rico because I should hate to put down my sword while that part of America remains in slavery."

Antonio Maceo

17. The Story Of Ana Roque

Her full name was Ana Roque de Duprey. She was born in the city of Aguadilla, Puerto Rico in 1853. Ana Roque de Duprey was one of the most remarkable women ever born in Puerto Rico.

Ana Roque was able to read, write and solve elementary problems of arithmetic at the age of three. At the age of nine she had mastered all there was to learn in the schools of those days.

At the ripe old age of 11, Ana Roque de Duprey was a supplementary teacher in one of the few schools that we had in Puerto Rico at that time.

When Ana was informed there was no textbook to teach geography, she went to work and wrote a book on universal geography. She also wrote a book on "The Botany of the Antilles" and many other books, pamphlets and papers including 32 novels.

Ana was perhaps the only woman in all San Juan who had a telescope on the roof of her house. Her researches in astronomy were recognized by "The Astronomical Society of France," that made her an honorary member.

When feminism started to spread over England and the United States, Ana Roque was instrumental in bringing to Puerto Rico the first currents of the women's rights movements as understood in those early days. Ana Roque was the founder of the first Puerto Rican feminist society. In 1917 she founded "La Mujer del Siglo XX" (Twentieth Century Woman), the first magazine to deal with women's problems in Puerto Rico.

Thus, Ana Roque had a number of "firsts" in Puerto Rican history. She was our first astronomer, the first newspaper woman. She was the first woman to be made doctor "Honoris Causa" by a Puerto Rican university. Ana Roque was also made honorary President of the "Puerto Rican Association of Women Voters" of which she was one of the founders.

This aspect of women's rights—woman's right to vote—was one to which Ana Roque dedicated many years of her life to make a reality.

In 1929 the Puerto Rican legislature passed a law giving Puerto Rican women the right to vote. Since then many women have been elected mayors of big cities, including Puerto Rico's capital which is headed today by the very well known woman Mayor Felisa Rincon de Gautier. Women had been elected judges. One of them, a member of the legislature, had presided over that important body.

Most of these achievements were the result of women's rights movements started around the second decade of the present century, inspired and directed by women like Ana Roque de Duprey.

When Puerto Rican women, for the first time, were given the right to vote in 1929, Ana Roque, then in her late 70's, made herself ready to go out and vote. She always had said one of the greatest thrills in her life, one of her most precious fulfilments would be the day when she could go out and exercise her civic right to vote as men had been doing for many years. As she was now very old and not so strong and healthy as she was in her younger years, she was brought out into the streets in a wheel chair, lovingly pushed by a dozen friendly hands to the voting place. Newspapermen and a great number of people were present. They wanted to tell the Puerto Rican world that they were present when Ana Roque de Duprey—the woman who had contributed so much to make women's right to vote come true—was herself exercising this right—one of the most important citizens' rights.

For many days and nights throughout many years, one of the most outstanding women in Puerto Rico's history, Ana Roque de Duprey—mathematician, astronomer, writer and fighter for women's rights—had thought about this moment in which she, herself, would be voting like any other citizen.

The cameramen with their cameras ready, the newspapermen, pencil and paper pad in hand, were alert to preserve for posterity this moment in the life of a woman who had done so much for Puerto Rican women.

People from all walks of life invaded the polling place to see Ana

Roque in the act of performing one of the greatest ambitions of her life: to vote, just like a man.

But Ana Roque was never able to realize her great ambition. For she had forgotten to register. In those early years of the 1930s, as now, you could not vote if you did not register. You must register in order to vote.

Ana Roque, in her immaculate black dress and her white pique collar, that she liked to wear so much, was taken in her wheel chair from polling place to polling place in the fruitless hope of finding out if her name was perhaps registered in some other place than the one in which she was supposed to vote.

It was all in vain. This woman, who had done so much to win the right to vote for Puerto Rican women, died soon after in 1933, at the age of 80, without ever being able to vote in her whole life. She had forgotten to register.

18. Pisagua*

Pisagua is not the name of a fancy summer resort somewhere in the tropics, with a clear blue sea and playful waves competing to be the first to arrive and kiss the sunny sandy shores.

Pisagua is a concentration camp in one of the most inhospitable spots in Chile. There the present Chilean government, under the presidency of Carlos Ibanez del Campo, and by the indirect order of the American copper and nitrates interests, keeps hundreds of Chilean labor leaders, rank and file workers and intellectuals today because they have dared to struggle for higher standards of living and a national democratic front of the Chilean people against the joint exploitation of the Chilean reactionary clique and American imperialism.

Let us recall briefly how, for example, Volodia Teitelboim, novelist and author of famous studies on the development of capitalism in Latin America and one of Chile's most outstanding lawyers and intellectuals was brought to Pisagua.

Raquel Weitzman, Volodia's wife and a lawyer in her own right, writes that one day, very early in the morning, they heard knocks at their door. They waited. The knocks were repeated. As they opened the door, agents of the Chilean Department of Investigation swarmed in and sat in the parlor as if they were the owners of the apartment. Raquel asked what they wanted. They answered that they came to take Volodia Teitelboim, her husband, into custody. When Raquel Weitzman asked for the usual judicial order of arrest, the agents said that they had none.

No matter how many inquiries were made by his wife and friends during the next few days, Volodia's prison whereabouts were kept secret until, finally, his wife was notified that Volodia was in Pisagua.

---

* This essay appeared in the *Daily Worker* on March 26, 1956 while Carlos Ibanez del Campo was still President of Chile.

In the same way Clotario Blest, Ernesto Miranda, Arman Aguirre, Juan Vargas Puebla and many other national and provincial leaders of the "CUT"—"Central Unica de Trabajadores" —the central union of Chilean workers and greatest unifying force in Chilean life today, have been taken to Pisagua, to Maullin, to Los Muermos, and many other concentration camps in Chile.

Pablo Neruda in his poem "The Men of Pisagua," tells us that: "It will be the honor of tomorrow to have been thrown in the sands of Pisagua."

Volodia Teitelboim in his unfinished book on Pisagua, says that the place is "like seeing hanging at the depth of the surrounding hills, a cobweb and in the middle of it, death."

While the Chilean government keeps in concentration camps the flower of the working class and its intellectuals, and while our travelling Secretary of State, John Foster Dulles, visits ten Asian countries in seventeen days, in a rather tardy effort to apply more dollar brakes to those countries' movements toward final liberation from colonialism, there are concentration camps like Pisagua in all the dictator-government countries in Latin America from Tierra del Fuego in Argentina to Guatemala and Santo Domingo in the Central and Caribbean areas of America.

In Indo-Afro-Spanish America, a great part of the best of its democratic leadership is lingering today in medieval prisons and concentration camps, their cries for justice unheeded by their government and by our own, so solicitous about going after the very smell of "force and violence" anywhere outside Alabama, U.S.A. and the countries governed by the Wall Street-supported dictators.

Here are some of the things that we would like the Latin American Section of our State Department to investigate:

The denial of a free press to the Argentinian people. Notwithstanding the gesture of the restoration of *La Prensa*, the publication of the working class press continues to be forbidden, from the Communist papers *La Hora* and *Nuestra Palabra* to *Vocero*, organ of the Argentinian peace movement, *Mujeres Argentinas* and *Juventud,* publications respectively of the women and youth movements in Argentina. The Argentinian government goes so far as to bring pressure and forbid the printing establishments to print them under any conditions. So, some of these publications have been forced to appear in a clandestine manner.

We would like our State Department to make at least a gesture of protest about the unjust imprisonment of working class leaders known and loved all over Latin America, like the Argentinian Ruben Iscaro, member of the Executive Committee of the World Federation of Trade Unions, and inquire in what Argentinian concentration camp he is being unjustly imprisoned.

We would like our State Department to ask our Ambassador in Venezuela for information on the wanton killing of hundreds of High School pupils in the streets of Caracas, Venezuela, as reported in the *New York Times* of March 1, 1956.

Our Ambassador in Venezuela should also ask the Venezuelan dictator Perez Jimenez in what Venezuelan concentration camp he is keeping the great Venezuelan trade union leader Jesus Faria and other leaders of the Venezuelan people's movement.

We would like our government to inquire from the "de facto" government of Guatemala to what extent are the workers rights and democratic liberties concretely assured under the new Guatemalan Constitution promulgated this very month by their puppet Castillo Armas. We would like our government to ask Castillo Armas for the freedom of Bernardo Alvarez Monzon, Hugo Barrios Klee, Efrain Villastro, Mario Melgar and other Guatemalan people's leaders and the return to their country of all Guatemalan political refugees covered by the guarantees established in the new Constitution.

We could go on endlessly. But inasmuch as our State Department or any part of our government today is not going to protest any of these causes so much in line with the democratic tradition of the people of the United States, we might as well start doing the protesting ourselves, as individuals, and by making the organizations to which we belong cognizant of what is happening under these Latin American dictatorships that would not be able to stand alone one hour, if it were not for the direct support of Wall Street and the indirect support of our present Washington government.

No more Pisaguas in Latin Americal

19. Rivera Back In Mexico*

    Diego Rivera, the great Mexican painter and muralist is back in Mexico after a long stay in the Soviet Union. He went there to get medical and surgical treatment for his cancerous ailment.

    Diego Rivera gave his first newspaper interview in Mexico to Luis Suarez, representing *Espana Popular,* the important organ of the Spanish Republican left in exile in Mexico and all through the rest of Latin America. It is from Luis Suarez' interview that we are taking most of the notes inserted in this column.

    While Rivera was attending to the many details and official papers on the night of Wednesday, April 4 at the Mexican airport, a group of popular Mexican singers and guitar players were singing him a Mexican "corrido" in the airport waiting room: Some of the verses went like this:

> *Diego se fue para Rusia*
> *en busca de su salud*
> *y algunos sabios doctores*
> *lo curaron en Moscu.*
>
> *Lo curaron con cobalto*
> *que sirve para hacer bombas,*
> *pero alla saben usarlo*
> *para curar a los hombres.*

    A loose translation of the above stanzas will read something like this:

> *Diego went to Russia*
> *To look after his health*

---

* This essay appeared in the *Daily Worker* on May 8, 1956, before the death of the great Mexican artist.

And some learned doctors
Cured him in Moscow.
They cured him with cobalt
Which is used to make bombs
But they learnt to use it there
To do good to mankind.

Anyone who has listened and seen the power of improvisation of the Mexican street singers while singing their "corridos"—a sort of an improvised Mexican ballad—could gather from the two stanzas just quoted, the humor and meaning of the dozen other improvised quatrains of this Mexican people's form of popular song and poetry.

If only Luis Suarez of *Espana Popular* or someone else in Mexcio could send us some of the other verses that were not lost in the Mexican wind that night of April 4, at the Mexican airport!

We know that there are some capable voices, banjos and guitars in the U.S.A. that would like to spread this singing message of progressive science, of peace and brotherhood, further and further through the cities and plains of this republic.

In parts of the interview Diego Rivera declared: "It would be impossible to describe, unless you are a literary genius, the very fine treatment, the profound human tenderness and delicate sensibility in the care and therapeutic applications of the Soviet doctors and nurses." And then he added as if trying not to circumscribe these delicate manners to the medical profession alone: "The whole Soviet people are great in their moral and physical strength."

Then he continued: "I have a vivid sensation of returning not from another country, but from another planet in which humanity is living in history and already has completely left the prehistory phase in which we still live on this side in which capitalism continues to rule. If I did not have to pass through the surgical clinic of Dr. Frunkin, I would have died ignoring almost totally the height to which human solidarity could reach with a love and tenderness that is much further ahead than what we know in our biological and fraternal relations."

Diego Rivera made it clear that treatment in the twenty cancer clinics in Moscow is given equally to agricultural laborers, industrial workers, intellectuals, artists or high government officials. In other words the treatment that he received was not given to him because he was Diego Rivera, but because he happened to need it and, being in the Soviet Union, he was entitled to it like anybody else.

"I saw with my own eyes"—said the great muralist—"hundreds of cases that in the capitalist world would have been declared incurable because of lack of means."

Diego Rivera explained: "It is not a question of paradise or of a miracle, but of a human society that is at a very high level of development and, though only thirty-eight years after the Socialist Revolution, their system is at an interplanetary distance from the old capitalist system of exploitation of man by man in which we live."

Diego Rivera was in the Soviet Union before in 1927. He describes the tremendous changes that have occurred in all fields of endeavor in the USSR since then. "Of course they have some bad painters among the thousands of painters that they have," Rivera acknowledged. Then he continued: "But the Soviet painters have resolved the problem of really modern painting, that is, socialist painting, because after all, the only thing that we could call absolutely modern is Socialism." He finished by saying: "The man of this modern society demands a clear art, without disguise, depicting what he does, what he constructs and enjoys, without veils or subterfuges that are not needed at this late date. In short, socialist realism."

Some thirty years ago Diego Rivera was in New York. Some fifty or sixty of us Latin Americans were invited to listen to him and ask him questions. I still remember my questions—and his answers. It was a very lively discussion in which we all participated.

We are all very happy indeed this side of the Rio Grande, that the great Mexican painter and world-known muralist came back from the Soviet Union entirely recovered. His cure is a great triumph both for Soviet science and for world progressive art.

Let us rejoice with our brothers, the Mexican people, and repeat with them in gladness and delight:

> *Diego se fue para Rusia*
> *en busca de su salud*
> *y algunos sabios doctores*
> *lo curaron en Moscu.*

20. Trujillo's Fair Of Blood*

There have been full and half-page ads during the last few weeks in most metropolitan newspapers announcing the fair of "peace" of the "free world" now being held at the capital of the Dominican Republic.

Who organized this fair and what is its real purpose at this time? As a government of a country with a 1955 budget of $108,000,000, more than half of which was spent on the army and its huge secret police composed of gangsters and criminals dedicated to suppress all expression of free thought and democracy, it would be interesting to know how such a "government" takes a sudden liking to "peace" and goes all out organizing a fair for the countries of the "free world" and against communism.

First: who is this Rafael Leonidas Trujillo y Molina, the dictator and virtual owner of all property, all life and liberty in the Republic of Santo Domingo since 1930? Who is this lover of "peace" and of the so-called "free world?" Trujillo is, without doubt, the bloodiest dictator of all Latin America. And we don't have to enumerate them, these human beasts coddled and protected by our present Administration in Washington. The job of these dictators in Venezuela, Nicaragua, Guatemala, Cuba, Chile as well as Santo Domingo is to keep these countries "free" for Wall Street plunder, in which these dictators are like junior partners.

This man Rafael Leonidas Trujillo, head of the Trujillo clan in Santo Domingo, was convicted of forgery in 1918, for which he served six months in jail. During the 1916-1924 American occupation of the Dominican Republic, he spied on the patriotic defenders of the rights and liberties of the Dominican people. For this spying he was properly repaid by being named the head of the Dominican Constabulary. He conspired against the duly elected President Horacio Vazques, being instrumental in the

---

* This essay appeared in the *Daily Worker* on February 6, 1956, several years before Trujillo's assassination May 30, 1961.

murder of the vice-president of the republic and eventually usurp-
ing the presidential seat for himself. In 1937, while "president"
of the republic, he ordered the massacre of 20,000 Haitian agricultural workers. His friends in the seats of power in the nations
of the "free world" barred an international investigation of this
tremendous crime. His suppression of the strikes in 1943 and
1946 against the big sugar plantations is well remembered for
its cruelty and sanguinary sadism. Through his agents in
New York and all the capitals of the Latin American countries,
he orders the assassination of all those who oppose his inhuman
activities against his own people. Thus, to mention only a few,
the murder of Mauricio Baez and Pepi Hernandez in Havana,
Cuba, of Sergio Bencosme, and of Andres Requena, who was
murdered by Trujillo's agents on October 2, 1952 in the hallway
of 243 Madison Street, New York. Mr. Requena, a frequent visitor
to the Fourth Avenue second hand bookshops, was an author of
several books against Trujillo and the editor of the paper *Patria*, in
this city.

Trujillo had the effrontery to name his three-year-old son captain
of the Dominican Army. When he was 11 years old, he was
already Brigadier General, with the regular pay and prerogatives
of a general of the army. Trujillo has the arrogance to change
the name of the oldest city founded and inhabited by Europeans in
both Americas—the city of Santo Domingo founded in 1496—and
to place his own tainted name on that ancient and historical city
in whose beautiful cathedral the remains of Christopher Columbus
are kept and venerated.

And this is the man who is inviting the "free world" to visit
and join him in this fair of blood just being held in the Dominican
Republic. Trujillo the great "democrat," the sole owner of life,
liberty and property in that beautiful country, Trujillo has monopo-
lized all business and industries—milk, tobacco, cement, sugar,
hotels, insurance, commercial aviation. At the head of each of
these monopolies, he places one of his henchmen or member of
his numerous family. He placed his brother Hector as the current
President of the Dominican Republic. This is Rafael Leonidas
Trujillo, the great lover of "freedom," the "Benefactor of the
Fatherland" as he likes to be called. He and his "government" ask

you to visit his fair of "peace" and against communism. As Carleton Beals, the North American author of Latin American books wrote: "The Plaza Colon could be paved with the bones of his victims."

According to information received by us, the opening of the fair did not bring the grand response that Trujillo and his gangsters wanted.

Official propaganda expected about 20,000 foreign visitors and 100,000 Dominicans from all over the republic to be present at the inauguration. Notwithstanding the low prices of the airplane excursion tickets, only a few hundred foreign visitors were present. The rest of the visitors were members of official delegations.

In his inaugural speech, Trujillo poured out all his hate against Geneva and the socialist countries. One of his daughters was crowned as the Queen of the Fair with a crown valued at $100,000. Her 55-foot ermine cape, adorned with diamonds and rubies, together with the gowns of her ladies in waiting, cost over $300,000. Trujillo offered a banquet to the official delegation that, according to the Associated Press, cost him around $1,000,000. Imagine having a champagne fountain pouring out the precious liquor all during the banquet! An American newspaperman commented: "Just like an oriental fairy tale!" The sweat, blood and sinew of the Dominican people thrown down the drain of a champagne fountain!

What is Trujillo looking for with this fair? He is trying to buy a higher sugar quota from the North American sugar trust. He is trying to hide the real conditions of hunger and slavery of the Dominican people back of the glamorous ermine of his daughter's gown. He is crying "peace," "prosperity" and "democracy" in order to stop the rising international protest against his crimes and depredations.

International public opinion can stop Trujillo's aim with his fair of blood, by giving the true facts of the situation in Santo Domingo. Do that anywhere you go. Anywhere you write. Anywhere you speak.

Salud, brothers and sisters, workers and progressive intellectuals of Santo Domingo! You are not alone!

21. Something To Read

A piece of working class literature, a leaflet, a pamphlet, a progressive book or newspaper are precious things in colonial and semi-colonial countries under the repressive measures of dictators.

An old dilapidated, moody mimeograph that works when it chooses to do so is, in an oppressed colonial country, like a battery of presses in a great metropolitan newspaper.

We know of a town in a Caribbean country where there was only one copy of a very famous pamphlet. The pages of the pamphlet were carefully taken apart. Two pages were given to each person to be written by hand, thus reproducing about one dozen pamphlets that were used to start a class!

A working class paper or book is read and passed along until the cheap material on which these articles are usually printed starts tearing into all kinds of crazy angles and the printed word just disappears from what is left of the paper.

I know of a little town in another tropical country where one copy of *The Soviet Power*, by the Dean of Canterbury, was read by 68 persons who could hardly read: You can imagine the condition of the book when it was finally returned to its original owner.

Here, when we are through with a paper, we usually throw it away. In colonial and semi-colonial countries, where to get a copy of a working class paper is in itself an achievement, we usually pass the publication to somebody else who, in turn will place it in somebody else's hands after he or she finishes reading it.

The way in which the working class and the people in general read and support their papers in the colonial and semi-colonial countries is something that we have to admire. They have very little and a great deal of that very little is given to their paper.

Take for example *El Siglo*—The Century—the great Chilean working class daily paper. The Chilean workers and peasants as well as a great part of the Chilean middle class feel that *El Siglo* is their paper. Everything of interest to the workers—national and international—is fully covered by *El Siglo*. The section devoted to popular poetry written by working class poets from all parts of the country is one section of *El Siglo* that goes to the heart of the Chilean people.

This great Chilean people's paper just finished a campaign to raise five million Chilean pesos in one month. For a country like Chile with a working class being paid starvation wages by the American imperialist corporations and its Chilean counterparts, this is a considerable amount of money to be raised in one month.

Besides the well known methods of house parties, public meetings, collections, outings and so forth, *El Siglo* encouraged fund raising events based on the Chilean customs of the people. Sometimes the paper based itself on the festivities and customs of a particular part of the country, as a means of raising money.

As we said before, the Chilean peasant is very much exploited and therefore very poor. In this one-month fund raising campaign for *El Siglo* the paper's sympathizers organized a meeting in Valdivia in the southern part of Chile. An old woman very humbly dressed came to the meeting hall and sat unobtrusively somewhere in a corner. As the meeting was coming to an end she got up and said:

"This time I have very little to offer for the fund raising campaign. Only this." And advancing toward the front table, she carefully placed on it one chicken egg. Then she walked back to her seat in the corner.

The silence was broken at last by a voice.

"Let us auction the egg! Let us auction the egg!"

And this was done. The egg brought at auction a considerable amount of money.

22. Origin Of Latin-American Dances
(According to the Madison Avenue Boys)*

A few Fridays back Ed Murrow took us all to visit Xavier Cugat and his wife Abbey Lane at their apartment at the Waldorf, on Murrow's "Person to Person" program.

This program is, with very rare exceptions, of a very high quality. Through Ed. Murrow we have gone into the homes of people like Grandma Moses, Ernie Ford of "Sixteen Tons" fame, and listened to what they've had to say about their own field of work. This is aside from Murrow's longer visual reports on Israel and Egypt and many other European filmic news feats that have brought his "See It Now" program well-earned commendation. His report on John Kasper's racist campaign against the Negroes in the South will be long remembered by all democracy loving Americans as a job well done for truth and justice. Also through Ed Murrow, we had the pleasure of accompanying the great artist, trumpet player and popular bandleader Louis Armstrong through most of the countries of Europe. We travelled with him, thanks to Ed Murrow's cameras, on buses, airplanes and trains. My heart was full of joy and enthusiasm at seeing with how much love and warmth Louis Armstrong and his band were received by thousands of his white admirers on train platforms and dance halls all over Europe.

But the night that we visited the Cugats with Ed Murrow some Fridays back, we received quite another impression. Maybe this program was decided upon in a hurry without much preparation. Maybe in his search for a sponsor, which all new shows on television are anxious to get, a few fundamentals were forgotten for the moment that unfortunately thwarted the very aims of the program.

----
* Madison Avenue is the place where all the big publicity and public relations firms have their offices.

For example, this is what the Cugats had to say on the origin of the merengue, the dance from Santo Domingo, so popular today in every dance hall in New York.

It seems that an Irish captain with a peg leg arrived in Santo Domingo. As he could not dance like everybody else, having to drag his wooden leg with him over the dance floor, the Irish sea captain started to dance one-sided giving a lame effect to his dancing. From then on, all the dancers of Santo Domingo followed the way the Irish captain with the peg leg danced the merengue!

Whether all Dominican dancers proceeded to cut off one of their legs, providing themselves with peg legs in order to more faithfully imitate the Irish sea captain, the Cugats did not say.

I suppose Trujillo is following the Irish captain's example with the people of Santo Domingo. Only instead of cutting the bodies of the Dominican people from their legs down, he starts to cut from their heads down.

Another thing that the Cugats or their script writers from Madison Avenue forgot to explain to us is how the Irish sea captain left his ship unattended while he travelled far from the sea shore into the interior of Santo Domingo, to the very mountains of Cibao for, according to all true merengue scholars (aside from those in the Madison Avenue publicity offices), that is where the merengue was born in Santo Domingo.

But let us pass on now to the origin of the tango according to Xavier Cugat and his wife or rather, according to their bright young publicity boys. Well, ladies and gentlemen, it happened in the following simple way:

The European waltz—the graceful, melodious 3/4 time waltz immortalized by the Strauss family—came to Buenos Aires, Argentina.

The Argentinians just could not grab the intricacies of the waltz time—one, two, three,—one, two, three,—that was just too, too difficult for them. As they went back to their ranchos in the Argentinian pampas, they tried to remember that new complicated waltz time—one, two, three, one. . . . They tried very, very hard but—poor people—for the life of all the cows and bull herds in

Argentina, they just could not remember the complicated dance. One, two. . . . In their effort to remember the waltz they hit on the "less difficult" dance we now call the tango. And that is the way it happened.

If they would only have taken the trouble to consult the 14th edition of the Encyclopedia Britannica, volume 21, page 786, they would have read there that the tango "probably originated with the African Negroes." But, of course, that does not sound, shall we say, too romantic, too picturesque. Cugat and his wife, being familiar with the Spanish language, could have consulted Argentinian authorities on this matter. Vicente Rossi's "Cosas de Negros" for example. This book is subtitled: "The origin of the tango and other folkloric matters of the Rio del Plata region in Argentina." They would have found there, that the European waltz had nothing to do with the origin of the tango, but that the Negroes in Argentina—the very same Negroes, slaves and free men who together with the white working class in 1806-1807 stopped the English from taking Buenos Aires and making Argentina another English colony, had very much to do with the origin of the tango. (The rich left Buenos Aires to its fate, going to their safe "estancias" away from the coast.) Cugat would have found in Rossi's exhaustive work on the tango and in many other Argentinian books on this subject, that the tango originated with the Argentinian Negroes at the beginning of the last century.

The tragedy of this, shall we say, glamorized "origin" of the Latin American dances according to Cugat and his brain boys is that, like H. L. Mencken's essay on the origin of the bath tub, this misinformation gets into reference books as honest to goodness truths. "Did not maestro Cugat, the leader of a famous orchestra, say so himself on television? What more proof do you want, man?"

We don't have to add that none of this speaks too highly for the respect, real love and seriousness with which Latin American music and culture in general are considered by those who should know better in these United States.

23. Hollywood Rewrites History

A few years ago some sailors of the United States Navy visiting Cuba climbed to the very top of the statue of Jose Marti in Havana. From the peak of the monument the sailors started to do pirouettes, twirling around and round and dancing all over the marble statue.

The people of Havana became very much incensed. The Cuban police saved the sailors from being lynched by the outraged masses gathered and waiting for them to come down to the base of the monument.

Cuba protested to the Navy Department and to the United States government. The American ambassador in Cuba laid a flower offering at the base of the statue and everything was treated by the U.S. papers as the pranks of innocent youth on a tropical holiday, instead of branding it for what it was—a reflection of U.S. imperialism's supremacist attitude toward small nations.

In the same vein, a supposedly responsible studio like Warner Brothers tackles such a theme as the struggle for Cuban independence from Spain, distorts the hitsory and geography of Cuba and presents Marti as a fat, contented, richly dressed man, living in a sumptuous palace in Haiti years after he fell at Dos Rios in the cause of Cuban independence. That is really taking the history and heroes of the Cuban people, and making it the material for one of those Hollywood super dupers in gaudy colors in which the eternal triangle of two men and a beautiful woman supersedes all truth and all historical honesty.

"Santiago," a Warner Bros. film, now being shown in some of the neighborhood theatres is such a tawdry monstrosity.

"Santiago" rides rough-shod, not over just one monument in a Havana public square—but over all Cuban history.

To present the great Jose Marti, who lived one-third of his life during the last century in poverty and want in New York City, as living in a magnificent castle full of tapestries and servants, while the Cuban people were fighting in their valleys and mountains against the oppressive Spanish government, is like presenting George Washington in his Virginia mansion, surrounded by servants and all the comforts of life, while the patriots of 1776 were hungry, ragged and cold in the snow-covered grounds of Valley Forge, fighting for independence against the oppressive English government.

Jose Marti never had a mansion or a hut of his own. Needless to say he never had slaves.

The glorious history of the Cuban Revolutionary Party, with its Puerto Rican section, both of which were organized by the Cuban and Puerto Rican workers and intellectuals living in Key West, in those days—the Cuban Revolutionary Party, the acknowledged leader and organizer of the Cuban Revolution of 1898—is completely ignored.

The tremendous role played by the Cuban and Puerto Rican cigarmakers in New York, Philadelphia, Tampa and other cigar manufacturing centers is just dismissed with a passing remark. Its honorable place in Cuban history is taken in this picture by a bunch of American contraband gun-runners led by Alan Ladd and by another bunch of American hi-jackers fighting it out with the Alan Ladd group, for lust and money, from the wilds of Florida to the very doors of Santiago, a city that never appears in the picture.

The heroic figures of Marti and Maceo, the heroic deeds of the Cuban people and the Cuban and Puerto Rican patriots like general Rius Rivera, the first military adjutant to General Maceo and the Puerto Rican poet Pachin Marin, who gave his life for Cuban independence in the Cuban manigua, are dumped into the Hollywood ash can and replaced by the most fantastic, flashy, supercolossal misinterpretation of Cuban history, adding to it all the sex appeal of the young Italian actress Rossana Podesta acting the part of a mythical Cuban Joan of Arc and the superman feats of Alan Ladd, a West Point graduate dishonorably discharged from the U.S. Army who, not only became the arms provider but also the brilliant strategist and ambuscade expert for the Cuban Revolution.

We understand that Hollywood's next Latin American film will be on Bolivar. After seeing "Santiago," and reading about the recent Bolivar "conference" in Panama, we could only say: Poor Bolivar! Hollywood's arrogant disregard for Latin American history and culture is just amazing, to say the least.

But, to continue—all these Hollywood high jinks in "Santiago" are richly seasoned with high sounding phrases about honor, duty and country, and cheap tear jerking scenes of the kinetoscope era. The sweet little boy who was killed by the Spanish soldiers seemed to die with a knowing smile on his lips as if he were just about to die laughing at the fakery of it all.

Just to surmise, as this picture does, that the cause of Cuban independence and the cause of the pro-slavery Confederate South were one and the same thing is historically false.

To see the captain of the gun-running ship dressed in all his Confederate splendor, and the ship itself, a ridiculously unseaworthy river boat with circular side oars, looking like old fashioned electric fans, rescued from the props for a "Show-Boat" show, gives the whole picture a back drop better suited for an opera-comique than a monumental saga on Cuban history.

"Santiago" is the lowest point yet reached by Hollywood in ignorance and arrogance against Cuba and all Hispanic American culture.

We think it would be wrong to dismiss our review of "Santiago," the film on Cuba's war for independence produced at the Warner Brothers studios, without pointing out the almost irreparable harm that such a picture could do on a world-wide scale.

We would like to point out further that all the Cuban historians, writing for years in every language of the globe, will not be able to undo the damage done to Cuban history and this picture's distorted presentation of the Cuban people on a world scale.

"Santiago" will be shown to millions of people all over the world. And to millions of these people—especially the very young ones—Jose Marti will remain a bloodthirsty soldier who kept an account of the many thousands of Spaniards that he killed and wounded.

Together with this film, thousands of so-called "comic" books, based on "Santiago" have been printed by the Dell Publishing House, Inc., 261 Fifth Avenue, New York City, to further perpetuate the errors on Cuban history and character in the minds of millions of readers. In this tragic "comic" book, Maceo—the "Bronze Titan," as the Cubans are so fond of calling him, is presented as a white man.

After pictures like "Zapata" and "Santiago" we can only hope that these Hollywood vulgarizers and distorters, without the least bit of respect for the history and culture of our Latin American nations, won't lay their bovine eyes upon epic themes like the Aztec struggle against Cortes' conquest of Mexico, or Sandino's fight against American imperialism, or Hostos' crusade for Latin American culture, education and liberty throughout the Americas. Unfortunately Bolivar has already been marked for the Hollywood pillory.

Let us struggle with our voices and our pens and all the media still left in the people's hands for another Hollywood period like that of the writers, artists, directors and producers in the tradition of the "Hollywood Ten."

We are informed that the writers, artists and the whole Cuban people are in an uproar against the showing of this film "Santiago." Petitions have been sent to the government asking that this picture be banned from the Cuban movie houses.

We hope that this protest will be picked up by all the people of Latin America and the rest of the defenders of truth and honesty in the arts throughout the whole world. It is the least we can do to stop Hollywood from arrogantly debasing the character and deeds of our great men and the entire history of our Latin American countries.

24. Chinese Opera In Latin America

Practically every country in the world has been visited by some major group of the musical, dramatic or sports world of the Soviet Union, China or the people's democracies.

We read with joy about the concerts of the Boston Symphony in Leningrad and Moscow and of the positive reactions of the Russian audiences toward the fine musicianship of this—one of the really great world symphony orchestras.

The performances of the American musicians of the Boston Symphony in the socialist countries serve to confirm something we knew from way back: that there is no such thing as an iron curtain in the Soviet Union and the other socialist lands. But when we read about the teams in almost all fields of sports, of the outstanding figures in science and the arts and all the famous artistic groups visiting other countries from the socialist world, it becomes clearer to me that we have in the United States a "Fingerprint Curtain" that is barring the American people from seeing and hearing the great sport, dramatic and musical organizations of the Soviet Union, China, and the rest of the Socialist world.

We have been following with great interest and enthusiasm the tour of the Peking Opera Company of the Chinese People's Republic all through Latin America. This unique opera organization consists of around 100 singers, actors and musicians. The most famous Latin American critics as well as the South American people in general are raving about each and every performance of this representative group of the Chinese opera.

The late president of Chile, Carlos Ibanez del Campo, his wife, Mrs. Graciela Letelier de Ibanez, as well as five members of his cabinet were present at the first performance of the Chinese opera at the Municipal Theatre in Santiago, Chile.

On Thursday, August 23, a delegation of the Peking Chinese opera made an official visit to Cardinal Jose Maria Carlo Rodriquez, the head of the Chilean Catholic Church. The delegation was headed by Chu Tu Nan, the general director of this Chinese opera

organization and president of the Chinese Committee for Cultural
Relations With Foreign Countries.

During their "day of rest" most of the members of the Chinese
Opera Company were busy learning about music and the other
arts in Chile. Its artistic director, Chao Feng, gave a lecture on the
Chinese Theatre to a group of Chilean actors at the "Chilean Ex-
perimental Theatre." Then Chao Feng gave another lecture to the
general public at the "Antonio Varas Theatre" also in Santiago,
Chile. Then the whole Chinese group went to visit the theatre of
the Catholic University of Chile. This was followed by a reception
at the Chilean Newspaper Club.

After the end of this "day of rest" Chu Tu Tan, the General
Director summed up the collective impression of the whole group
with these modest words: "Today we have been learning from the
Chilean artists and people."

Egemont, well known music critic of the Chilean daily *El
Siglo* has this to say after seeing a performance of the Chinese
opera:

"Now we know why the critics of the European countries have
proclaimed the performance of the Chinese Opera of Peking as one
of the most beautiful spectacles in the world. All that fantasy could
imagine is very little compared with the artistic reality that the
Peking Opera offers us. Adjectives like superb, magnificent,
stupendous, the most admirable and expressive words in the Spanish
language used to convey our feeling in similar cases, mean very
little to qualify such a multiple show without equal in the world."

Then he adds: "The Peking Opera is without doubt, the most
pure manifestation of artistic culture of one of the countries with
the most ancient civilizations in the world."

Let us struggle, all together, to lift our "Fingerprint Curtain"
and give warm greetings from our shores to the many sports,
dramatic, musical and other artistic organizations from the Soviet,
Chinese and the peoples' democratic countries.

It will be a great day for peace and co-existence when the President of the United States, his wife and half of his cabinet will be
present in the National Theatre in Washington, enjoying an evening of Chinese Opera presented by the Peking Opera Company.

25. Jose

We will call him Jose. Which, of course, is not his name. I knew him thirty years ago with a guitar in his hands. Today if you call on him in the basement apartment back of the courtyard, after you pass through that dark arched passage way you will probably still find him with a guitar in his hands. Before you get to his little apartment behind the big boiler room of this big old apartment building, you might be listening to some guitar music coming as if from a distance. That most probably would be coming from Jose and his guitar.

Who taught him to play the guitar? Nobody. He picked it up himself, bit by bit, adding a chord today and another tomorrow until you doubt if there is anything else Jose has to learn about guitar playing. About the mood, the feeling, the art, the "mysteries" of guitar playing, that is something else. Segovia continues to discover those guitar mysteries even to this day.

Jose has taught himself a number of instruments. He sort of falls in love with them. He goes to a second hand book store and buys a book on the method of learning the instrument. Then he starts studying by himself until he practically masters the darn thing.

That was the way Jose taught himself harmony. The first book he bought on harmony cost him twenty-five cents. Now he has quite a library on harmony. All second-hand books. From the looks of some of those books on music that Jose has, I bet some of them are sixth or seventh hand.

I loaned my good friend a history of music some three or four years ago. I don't dare to ask him to return it to me. I just don't have the heart. Jose likes to read about all aspects of music. Especially Puerto Rican music.

Every two or three months on a Saturday night I tell my wife that I am going to Jose's. She knows that I will be coming home between three and four in the morning. Jose likes to talk as much as he likes music. Those are his two favorites loves: music and talk, talk and music. When you visit him, he gets his guitar, tunes it, plays a few chords for just two minutes or so. Then he starts to talk about old Puerto Rican musicians and composers, about some great Puerto Rican musicians whom he knew in his youth. He relates some amusing or tragic anecdote about the particular figure he is talking about. All through this one-sided conversation his guitar has not left his lap. When he feels like making a pause in his rapid-fire way of talking, he tunes his guitar again, improvises something for a few minutes—something beautiful and lost in the air—and then continues to talk.

How Jose likes to talk! I don't know what he likes best: to talk or to play the guitar. It would be a toss-up.

I would reach Jose's place around nine. Then I'd have to listen to him talk until around eleven, with a phrase here or there that he allows me to throw in just to keep up the appearance that what we are having is a conversation and not a monologue. By about eleven we are concentrating on Jose's guitar music.

One of the things that my guitar-playing friend likes to do is to take a waltz for example—he plays it like a waltz—then he says: "Now you will hear this waltz as if it were a tango." Then you will hear the same music played like a fox trot, and a march, and a rumba and he goes along playing the same waltz music in all those different forms. Finally he would say: "And now I will play it as a funeral march." After he finishes it that way, we bury the waltz for the night.

All this time Jose's wife is preparing a refreshment of Quaker oats, vanilla, sugar, ice cubes and milk. She knows I like that kind of refreshment. Without asking Gallup to take a poll on it, I know that nobody can prepare that Puerto Rican refreshment better than Carmen, Jose's wife. When she hears the waltz being done as a funeral march, she is readying things and pouring her delicious refreshment into her spotlessly clean glasses. She will come from the kitchen into the parlor and, tray in hand, she will go around and offer a glass to each and every one present. As we enjoy the refreshment and relax, Jose will resume his "conversation."

After about twenty minutes of "conversation" mostly by my guitar-playing friend, he would again transfer his guitar from his lap—where it has been all this time—to his hands. "Now you will listen to how the Puerto Rican twangs the guitar." And in a "Guaracha" or "plena" form he will give a wonderful interpretation of Puerto Rican guitar playing that reminds you of your days as a youth on your native island—Puerto Rico—hung like a multicolored tropical hammock between the Atlantic Ocean and the Caribbean Sea.

Jose would continue. "Now you will hear how the Cubans play the guitar." And he would play a Cuban slow bolero, finishing with a rapid rumba. Just like a Cuban playing the guitar "And this is how the Argentinians play." Jose would go into an Argentinian tango, singing it at the same time with a voice—a cross between Louis Armstrong's and Martha Raye's—that has a human quality, a warmth to it like—like Louis Armstrong and Martha Raye. Jose will finish these imitations with interpretations of all the different ways the guitar is played in Mexico for bambas, huapangos, corridos and rancheras until you really think Jose might not be Puerto Rican at all but an honest to goodness Mexican guitar player somehow gone astray from some Mariachis orchestra into the wilds of New York City.

While he plays I keep wondering how many Joses are lost in the basements and top floors of New York City, with nobody telling them that they have talent, that they are perhaps geniuses. That they are a product of that ever self-renewing admirable mass of beauty and ugliness, enthusiasm and frustration we call the people.

Jose taught himself to dance. I mean to dance professionally. So by his ability to play many instruments, to sing in a sort of a way, and to dance, he landed jobs that took him to Puerto Rico and to some of the famous summer resorts as a musician and a dancer.

The Puerto Ricans had a friend in New London, Connecticut. An American Negro, a lover of Latin American music and Puerto Rican food. Every year on his birthday, our friend in New London

used to invite thirty to forty Puerto Ricans from New York to his
home. When he came down to New York, he had to spend most
of his time making the rounds from Puerto Rican home to Puerto
Rican home where he was received with the same friendliness
with which he received us when we went to New London.

The last year that I went to Connecticut for my friend's birthday, he was excusing himself because he had been unable to get
a "Conjunto"—a small group of Latin American musicians from
New York—to entertain his guests and give them some "live" music,
instead of having to dance to records as we were doing. We
were more than satisfied with everything. Plenty of food on long
tables along the hallway up to the kitchen, a variety of drinks and
the latest of Latin American and North American popular music,
plus a progressive atmosphere.

Around eleven o'clock in the evening our New London friend
started to excuse himself again for having been unable to get a
few Latin American musicians from the city.

"To think that while we are dancing to records, you have
"S.O.B.'s" in the big hotels all throughout the mountains dancing to the best "Conjuntos" and the best orchestras that money
can provide. And here we are dancing just to records." Our
friend continued: "Look at this New London paper--hotels, summer resort hotels—all with orchestras. Jesus, look at the advertisement of this big hotel in the paper. They are headlining a full
fledged Cuban 'Conjunto' for their dance and floor show tonight."

"What did you say about a Cuban Conjunto," I asked while
I kept dancing.

"A Cuban 'Conjunto' and floor show is playing at the Hotel—
tonight."

"How far is that hotel from this house?" I inquired from my
New London friend. He answered me with another question.
"What are you thinking of doing, Jesus?" "Please get that hotel
telephone number. When you do, say that you want to speak
to the leader of the Cuban orchestra."

My friend opened his mouth as if to say something, but then
on second thought he just went to the phone. He got the leader
of the Cuban musical group. Something told me that where there

is a Cuban "Conjunto" playing it must have some Puerto Rican musicians in it. So I took the phone and in a very natural voice I asked. "Will you let me speak to the Puerto Rican musician, please?" "Which one of them?" answered the voice on the other end. "We have—the bongo player and—the guitar player and Jose who plays bass and dances in the floor show."

"That is the one I want to speak to, Jose." I was shooting an arrow to hit a star a million miles away. And the arrow hit the star right at its center. As soon as he uttered the first word I knew he was Jose, my friend from Brooklyn.

"Hello, cabo." That is the way Brooklyn Puerto Ricans address each other if they have been living in "Dodgertown" over forty years.

"So this is a small world after all! Is it not, cabo?" Then I added: "How would you guys like to come over to a terrific party after you finish your last show in that joint you are playing tonight? You can relax with *real* people, have *real* food, play and dance a bit before you go to bed. We will drive you back and forth."

While I was speaking over the phone, dancing stopped. Somebody said: "What a nerve this guy has!"

"How about it, Jose?"

"Let me see what the boys have to say." After a few minutes Jose came to the phone. "OK, Jesus, be here with cars at one o'clock tonight." When I told the party that we were going to have some light Cuban music with "live" musicians from one of the big hotels in the mountains, they could hardly believe it.

Our friend, the owner of the house, for whom the birthday party was being given, who knew the side roads and byways of the mountains, was driving the first car. I was in the front seat with him. Another of the cars that had come from New York accompanied us.

The hotel was one of the tremendously big ones with a lot of grounds and buildings to it. It took us a few minutes to find out just where the musicians' sleeping quarters were. When we got there, they were just changing from their tuxedos to their ordinary suits.

We drove back to New London. And that is how we got some live Cuban music and musicians in the mountains, to help us celebrate the birthday party of our Negro friend in New London.

Jose has a very good musical memory. Sometimes he starts remembering Puerto Rican lullabies that have been forgotten or replaced by others. Using his guitar he illustrates songs and just musical phrases that he heard on a sugar cane plantation many years ago. These he learned from the West Indian Negro laborers who used to come to work on the Puerto Rican sugar cane plantations when Jose was still a child.

Here is another pastime we indulge in when I go to visit Jose. He plays one of his original songs. I take a piece of paper and a pencil and write words to his song as he endlessly repeats for me his musical composition bar by bar.

When I think I have the words according to Jose's music, I know the melody almost by heart. Then I ask him to accompany me, while I sing the words to his music. We look for a suitable title according to the words that I have written. Then we call it a "plena," "merengue" or "mambo," according to the rhythm of the music.

Other times I hear a phrase in the subway or bus while I am riding surrounded by Puerto Rican people. I make a mental note. I say to myself: "That phrase is a good title for a 'merengue.'" Next thing I will work on the lyrics for a merengue with the phrase as a title. It serves me as good relaxation on my one evening home after supper time. When I finish the lyrics I place them in an envelope and send them to Jose.

I visit him once every two or three months. He seldom comes to my house, unless there is something important that he wants to discuss with me. My visits are long. After the customary two hours talkfest soliloquy by Jose, he gets his guitar and "surprises" me with the music of the "plena" or "merengue" for which I sent him the lyrics through the mail a couple of months before. Sometimes he even has the music paper ready with my words neatly hand printed underneath every one of his notes. When this happens we always agree that a copy of the music and words should be sent to Washington together with the copyright fee.

"That will be done tomorrow first thing," Jose would say. In the meantime, music and words are buried in one of Jose's multiple suitcases full of written music and second hand books. Some years after I ask: "And whatever happened to that piece we wrote, that we said we were going to send to Washington first thing in the morning to be copyrighted? A record should have been made of it a long time ago." And Jose will answer calmly, very calmly: "You, know, cabo, that piece must be with the other pieces we have written during the last few years in one of those suitcases under the bed." And there the thing will rest until I write another lyric and he writes the music to it and after he plays it to "surprise" me once, we promise each other that this one piece will *certainly* be sent to Washington to be copyrighted. But, as it happened a dozen times before, the new piece will go to accompany the others in one of the suitcases under his bed. This ridiculous musical vicious circle has been going on for years without having been broken once.

No, I am wrong. Jose broke this circle all by himself just for once.

He wrote a very catchy piece of dance music. As it required very few words, he wrote the short lyrics himself. It consisted of a phrase that is repeated time and time again.

Jose is of an almost naive nature, though he thinks he is very wise in the ways of the world. Instead of sending this new composition to Washington as we have *never* done, he gave it to a musician "friend" of his. The musician took it to a well known music publishing house, and it was copyrighted. But not in Jose's name but in the company's name.

The first time that he heard his latest composition on a record was when he was passing by a music record store and he listened to the music being blared into the sidewalk crowd from a microphone they had hanging from the door.

Jose went into the store and bought his record.

"That's my composition. I wrote that music."

The man back of the counter looked at him with doubt and disbelief all over his face. His only reply was: "That is the hit of the hour—everybody is buying it."

The dance hit was being bought right and left not only here but all over Puerto Rico and the rest of Latin America. There was not a Puerto Rican home or a Latin American bar and grill or restaurant without Jose's record included in the record machine. From the Broadway Palladium to the smallest hole in the wall in the Bronx, Manhattan and Brooklyn calling itself a dance hall, Jose's music filled the air with its catchy beat.

If I tell you the name of the record, you will say, if you are any kind of follower of Latin American dance music. "Of course—I heard it a hundred times if I heard it once . . ." But I just will not give you the name of the record, just as I am not giving you Jose's real name.

I was surprised to see Jose in my home one evening. It must be very important. As I said before, I usually went to his home. He seldom came to mine. "Cabo, I have been robbed." "How, Cabo?" "I wrote a dance number based on one of those tunes I heard from the West Indian sugar cane cutters in Puerto Rico during my childhood. I am sure I played it for you on my guitar many times . . ." "And what happened?"

"Well, I showed it to some musician friend of mine. He brought it to a music and record publishing firm. . ." "And?" "And they copyrighted and recorded it in their names. Today the record is a hit. In Puerto Rico alone they sold 30,000 records. The name of the song is—" As soon as he mentioned the name I knew it was a hit every Puerto Rican was whistling and everybody was dancing.

"But why didn't you come to me, as you have many times before?"

"I come to you now—just a little too late."

We wrote letters to music lawyers, to the record company, to Washington. After months of letter writing and telephoning, after thousands of records of his popular dance number were being sold throughout the United States and Latin America, after two or three imitations of his catchy tunes were also recorded, after piles of money were coined by Tin Pan Alley and by the imitators of Jose's best-selling record, the recording company sent my friend Jose a check as a sort of cover-up and insurance against a future legal litigation. The check was for $214.00!

A tune maturing in a man's head for over forty years. Then somebody appropriates it through legal skulduggery and they send the man who did it all, two hundred and fourteen dollars!

The great tragedy of it is that nothing could be done about it. At least for the present.

26. Sarah

Sometimes we work with people for years; we see them and talk to them every day. But we don't actually know them. Our knowledge of them is superficial and formal. We see the vase but are never curious about its contents.

How often do we take time out in our daily chores to really know and understand friends, workers, family relations, so that we can enjoy their company more, so that by deepening our knowledge of them we come to love and appreciate them more?

Take Sarah. Sarah is over 60 years young. She always has a smile to offer you. Her step is brisk and swift like a teen-ager. She is always humming songs for she is a great lover of music.

I still remember the day she showed me her mandolin. That instrument is the apple of her eye. She took her mandolin out of its leather case and very, very carefully, as if she were handling a newly born baby, she entrusted the instrument into my hands. The strings were turned too low. I started to tune the mandolin to a higher pitch. . . . It happened. One string broke leaving a lingering sound in the air. Sarah almost cried. She did not let me buy the string for her. She bought it and placed it on the mandolin herself.

Fortunately our acquaintance was ripe enough by that time to start being called a friendship and the broken string incident was soon forgotten.

Sarah loves music. She told me all about the long months of rehearsals of Beethoven's Fifth Symphony by the string instrument orchestra to which she belongs and their final performance of this symphony in one of the best known halls.

"I tell you, Jesus, it was something great. Our performance of Beethoven's Fifth Symphony. I was up there, on that big stage, with my mandolin, together with all the other amateur worker musicians."

Then Sarah made a great pause as if trying to relive that most important moment in her life. Then she continued: "And as we kept playing Beethoven's Fifth, the meaning of the whole symphony became clearer and clearer to me.

"You have, of course, heard Beethoven's Fifth? You remember the first three sharp notes, followed by a long one, like this: 'Ta, ta, ta, taaa.'" And here Sarah will give three short blows on top of the nearest table, hitting the long fourth blow with an air of finality. "For me, Jesus, that revives memories of an older period in my life—Russia of 1905.

"My family comes from Lithuania," Sarah continued, "which in those days was a province of Russia. Many abuses and injustices were committed against the Jews and the people in general. After the 1905 revolution was crushed, hundreds were thrown into jails. Pogroms against the Jews became more frequent.

"Before my father got up to go to the synagogue, my sister, dressed in peasant's clothing and barefoot, used to go into the countryside carrying a basket with hay at the bottom and inside the basket, hundreds of leaflets covered with layers of eggs. My sister used to distribute these leaflets along the countryside telling the people to organize against greed and injustice. For that, my sister got six months in jail."

Sarah continued. "The terrific struggle that you hear in the first movement is all the picture of the 1905 revolution. Then comes the second movement. The music here is calm, direct, profound. Which shows you the calm, direct, methodical organization of the forces that were left and had not become disillusioned after the 1905 defeat. The beginning of the third movement gives you that feeling that great things are being prepared until the French horns followed by the strings announce the breakthrough of the working class in a glorious jump into the future. . . . The fourth movement is 1917, after which we see the great realization of brotherhood and happiness among men as socialism triumphantly flourishes all over the world."

You have to agree with me that Sarah's interpretation of Beethoven's Fifth symphony puts to shame all the analyses ever given of this work in all the courses in music appreciation from the Jefferson School of Music to the Juilliard School.

I have a hunch that when Beethoven was writing the Fifth, he had Sarah's interpretation of it in his mind.

And so this is Sarah. A worker. One tiny little grain of the salt of the earth.

27. Marcelino

The other evening my wife was in a pensive mood. "It is two years today since Marcelino died," my wife said. "And it seemed just like yesterday," she added. I agreed. For people like Marcelino remain with us—in our minds and hearts—many years after they are dead.

Marcelino was a Puerto Rican who belonged to the world working class. He left Puerto Rico very young, hiding in a ship. Since youth he seemed to have a notion that ships, trains and such were, if not his, the property of his entire class—the working class. For whenever he felt like going anywhere he hopped on a train or boat and off he went.

The people in charge of these transportation media seemed to have a different idea. Marcelino was never provided with cabin or Pullman accommodations. Many a time he had to ride the train underneath the cars, just a little over the rails.

Living that way for many years Marcelino acquired a vast knowledge of life and a boundless experience in worldly things as he grew from a boy into a youth and from a youth into a man.

It was during the old IWW days in one of the tramp jungle camps alongside the railroad tracks somewhere in one of the western states, that Marcelino discovered the progressive movement. From there on he became another person. The vague notion he had in his youth that the working class was the source of all wealth and all power became a scientific certainty with him.

Marcelino became a seaman. He joined the union and went sailing to many ports on all the seven seas, adding more anecdotes and strange experiences to his life. Sometimes he stayed in different countries for months and for years: Panama, Peru, France, Spain and Italy, to mention just a few. This gave a queer accent to his Spanish. He lost most of the peculiarly Puerto Rican words and phrases that give a particular Puerto Rican dressing to our Spanish. Notwithstanding all this, Marcelino was Puerto Rican to the core.

Through the many years that I knew Marcelino, he always

repeated his anecdotes and experiences in the same way. This gave them a ring of authenticity.

When Marcelino came from a long voyage, the first thing he did was to come to the *Daily Worker* and give a donation to the paper. The donation was in proportion to the length of the trip. Then he made the rounds of all the progressive organizations. And he gave money to them for whatever cause they were raising funds at the time. Then he started giving dollars here and there until he himself had to ask for subway money to go to the union hall.

When he was blacklisted from ships and forced to stay ashore, Marcelino did not miss a picket line or a public meeting. If leaflets had to be distributed at the subway entrance, you could count on Marcelino. If a delegate was needed to complete a delegation to Albany or Washington, Marcelino was ready to be that delegate. If it was necessary to get up at five in the morning to do some work for the working class, Marcelino was there. Then, as he came in late at night, he always managed to struggle through a few pages of a pamphlet or a worker's paper, his failing eyesight notwithstanding.

Marcelino was a real son of the working class. He had an infectious laugh. It was a jolting laugh that went from a high pitch to a low pitch in just a few seconds. He laughed at the least laughable provocation, often laughing until he cried for sheer joy.

One thing that Marcelino had beyond all measure was his infinite confidence in the working class and the people. In that great period of fear from which we are just emerging,* when only very few people came to meetings, you could always count on Marcelino to be present.

His confidence in the ultimate triumph of the working class and the people extended to the four corners of the earth. When anybody started to get tired and just plain disillusioned, because Marcantonio was not re-elected to Congress or because a great progressive organization was forced to disband, Marcelino always

---

*Refers to the period of McCarthyite reaction which continued into the mid fifties.

was ready with a few examples of the great triumphs of the working class in some other countries. He took a global view of the people's struggles.

He always had trouble with his feet. When they became so bad that he could only walk with great difficulty, and when his eyes had to be operated upon, he hated to miss a mass meeting or a demonstration. Those who went were forced to describe it all and give a summary of each speech to Marcelino.

When he died there were large floral offerings from the Communist Party Club and the small social club around the corner, as well as from his union and dozens of friends and acquaintances. Everybody from left to right, was present at Marcelino's funeral.

Sometimes I wonder how Marcelino would have taken all this about Stalin's errors and the cult of the individual; of the transition to socialism and the interpretation and discussions of these and other matters all over the world. Well, I think that he would have read and pondered all these questions after he came back tired from picketing or distributing leaflets somewhere. He would, I am sure, have participated in any discussions organized around these questions wherever he had an opportunity to express an opinion. But he would keep up his activities, his contributions and confidence in the working class. For Marcelino knew that it is in the practice of what thousands like him do every day to advance the interests of the people, that the correct theory for the solving of the many problems that confront us will be discovered. When you are busy in the working class, you hardly find time and the inclination to become disillusioned.

And after all, it is the working class and the people who will write the final report.

28. Carmencita

My wife and I still remember the day when Carmencita, my mother-in-law, came from Puerto Rico to live with us.

She examined our apartment minutely but unobtrusively. The kitchen and two bedrooms. The parlor with rows of books more or less neatly tucked in home-made bookcases. And the books. She read every title, her myopic eyes very close to the bindings.

After she finished her thorough examination, she went to one of the front windows facing the street and looked pensively down at the people passing on the sidewalk a few stories below Carmencita stayed in that position for a long time. Then she called my wife to the room we had prepared for her and closed the door.

When my wife came out of their long conference, I was already in bed. She seemed preoccupied and nervous.

"What is the matter?" I asked as she dropped the comb with which she was fixing her hair.

"Carmencita," she said, "will not spend a second night under the same roof with you."

"Why?"

"Because . . . you are a pagan, a . . . materialist . . . an atheist . . . a—"

"How does she know all this," I interrupted, "when we have hardly spoken to each other?"

"She said she knows what you are because of your books, because there is not an image of a saint in our whole apartment. My mother said that a man with books like that should be named 'diablo' instead of Jesus like they named you."

As my wife went on with what her mother had said, I realized I had a problem on my hands seriously affecting the future of our family. What should I do?

Carmencita, or Tita, as we all knew her since our early days in Puerto Rico, was the living austere portrait of a medieval Catholic woman. Faith was her only guide. I remember how I used to tremble from head to foot when she caught me staring at her daughter, my childhood sweetheart, who would look out at me from the small window of their home in Puerto Rico.

Carmencita was erect then, over fifty and of a firm and stubborn character. Her profile had the lines of Dante's familiar marble bust, and she looked as if she wanted to send all infidels and such to the remotest depths of his Inferno.

Carmencita's eyes were commanding. Very seldom did she let her long, pale face reveal the slightest emotion. Her slim figure moved with the sure step of those who firmly believe they are going straight to heaven when they die. But under that rigid composure and fierce, almost defiant saintliness, there was a world of sentiment and love for the downtrodden that took me years to discover and really appreciate before she died.

The immediate problem was to convince Carmencita that people owning and reading such "horrible" books as the ones she saw in the parlor were not such bad people after all—in fact that she could live under the same roof with her daughter and myself for years and years.

Early next morning I went to a Catholic religious store. I asked to see an image of Jesus. I picked one that seemed to be very human. From there I went to the nearest Five-and-Ten and bought a framed picture of some fruits painted in very flashy colors. I threw the fruits away and placed the image of Jesus in the frame. Now it looked as if I had bought both image and frame in the same store.

I came home. My wife and mother-in-law were in the kitchen. I went in looking for the one-eared hammer that we had. I took a piece of thin wire, two small nails and a big one and went to Carmencita's room. At first Carmencita and her daughter heard my puttering and hammering without moving from the kitchen, but after a little while curiosity grew stronger than reserve. They came to the door just as I was hanging the picture on the wall at the head of her bed.

"How do you like it?" I asked blandly.

A faint glow of satisfaction appeared on Carmencita's face. Almost imperceptibly, her head nodded in approbation.

After supper we three took a walk around the neighborhood. I took pains to point out to her places and persons of interest, the customs and nationalities of the people in New York.

Came Sunday. I took Carmencita to St. Patrick's Cathedral. We entered through the right. I started asking her questions. "Who is that saint?" And she started explaining the causes and circumstances of his or her sainthood. I noticed that her brief biographical sketches coincided closely with the printed notes framed in front of every saint. We went from right to left of the church with her lecturing a few minutes at every pedestal. I was patient and respectfully attentive to every word. As we went out, we were greeted by the myriad peaceful doves on the wide steps of the cathedral and the hustle and bustle of the Fifth Avenue traffic a few feet ahead.

The great Prometheus in the water fountain was looking calmly at the semicircle of umbrella tables at the Radio City Cafe.

"If a couple of Negroes dared to sit at one of those tables, they would not be served," I remarked, pointing at the cafe in the round circle below.

"Why?" questioned Carmencita.

"Because Negroes are looked upon as inferiors in this country and are not given the same rights as the whites. And that goes for us Puerto Ricans, too."

"Strange," she said, "I thought this was a very democratic country."

I did not press the point. I rather let it rest and watched for any effect my words might have on Carmencita. After I pointed out casually that the Puerto Rican flag was not among the many adorning the Radio City Plaza, we went into the main building to see the frescoes.

I explained to Carmencita that originally a Mexican painter named Diego Rivera was contracted to do the frescoes. He started by painting a Negro and a white worker clasping hands and the figure of Lenin in the middle, with Lenin's hands touching the hands of both men. When the Rockfellers, the owners of Radio

City, took notice of what Diego Rivera was painting, they paid
him up in full and discharged him, removing what he had already
done.

"And who was this man Lenin that the painter selected to be
in the center?"

I explained as simply as I could. We kept on walking through
the main building until we reached the Sixth Avenue entrance.

In those unemployment days of the Thirties only an alley
separated the Home Relief office on Adams Street in Brooklyn and
our apartment.

The Workers Alliance used to organize demonstrations and sit-
down strikes inside the relief offices. Sometimes their members
would stay inside the relief offices all night, refusing to be ousted
from the premises.

Joe Hecht, one of the leaders of the Workers Alliance in
Brooklyn, used to come to our apartment to prepare coffee and
sandwiches for the sit-down strikers and talk of their rights to
relief and better conditions generally. Joe knew a little Spanish
and he and my mother-in-law grew to know each other pretty well.

Carmencita could not conceive how a "judí" could spend so
much time and risk jail and perhaps a beating trying to get help
for the Puerto Rican people. Joe and I sat down with Carmencita
to explain that there was something greater than nationality and
so-called "race"—and that is the conscious feeling and understanding of belonging to a class that unites us regardless of color and
nationality, without belittling the contributions and positive qualities of our particular nationality. Joe Hecht, the Jewish-American,
and the Puerto Rican looking for help at the relief offices, belonged
to the same class: the working class.

Another thing that my mother-in-law could not understand was
how it was that a very intelligent and capable fellow like Joe
was working for eight dollars a week—and not always that—
for the Workers Alliance, when he could very easily be earning five
times as much working at his own trade. Joe explained this to her
in his modest way. I helped him with his Spanish whenever he
could not find the right words.

After Joe finished one of his explanations, Carmencita used

to sit by the window and reflect for a long time while the voices from the picket line in front of the relief offices continued chanting the demands of the day.

For two or three weeks, Joe did not come to chat with us. We learned that he had received a terrible beating on a picket line. That upset Carmencita and all of us very much. Then one day Joe came with his head all bandaged. When Carmencita saw his condition she let go with her scant arsenal of nasty words in Spanish against the police who had beaten Joe so badly. Joe explained to my mother-in-law that the police were only the instruments through which the capitalists operated to crush the rising consciousness and demands of the workers.

Carmencita had a great admiration for Joe. She admired him more when he joined the Abraham Lincoln Brigade and left for Spain to fight against fascism.

I will say that Joe's leaving for Spain had something to do with inducing Carmencita to take part in the pilgrimage to Washington in which over a thousand women from New York alone went to protest the arms embargo against Republican Spain. She joined in picketing the White House together with hundreds of other women. When she came back, she gave us a comprehensive report in Spanish of everything she saw and heard. She added a very sound criticism of a few errors made on this historic trip to Washington.

It was a happy day in our apartment when Joe Hecht returned from Spain, bald and thin, but with a fluent mastery of Spanish and, of course, a greater clarity and understanding of the whole fight against war and fascism. Carmencita received him as she would her own son.

It was a day of great sorrow in our home, years later, when we got the news that Joe Hecht was killed attacking a Nazi machine-gun nest during the Second World War.

We have a custom in regard to the dead. For nine consecutive days after the funeral, prayers or "rosarios" are conducted in the home of the deceased's family. The rosario is a long and repetitious prayer full of Latin passages and needing a conductor who has, through long experience, mastered the consecutive order of

the rosary and the Latin interpolations. Most of the rosàrio con-
ductors do not know what they are saying in Latin.

In Puerto Rico it would be highly insulting to one of these
prayer leaders if a person even insinuated that she or he should
accept payment for the services. These last rites are supposed
to be a strictly pious act, free from any taint of money or presents.

Carmencita was an expert on rosario conducting. And she
always paid her own carfare and other expenses to the place where
the rosario was going to be held.

Thus, when she was invited to conduct some rosario and she
was informed that this whole tradition had been commercialized
here (the prayer leader being brought back and forth in a taxi
or automobile and dined and wined before or after each night of
praying, besides receiving payment or a small gratuity, she
dropped it all and refused to conduct any more rosarios as long as
she remained in the United States. She also objected very
strenuously to the fiesta character that has developed in New
York around this religious ceremony. We pointed out to her the
influence of the money-concept of life and culture that those who
control everything have forced on even the most revered customs
and traditions of the people.

Carmencita received further proof that our criticism of present-
day society was correct when she went with her honor diplomas,
fraternal degrees and credentials to a worldwide fraternal organization to which she had dedicated many years of her life in
Puerto Rico. First she was informed that this organization,
preaching equality and brotherhood all over the world, was divided
between whites and Negroes here in the land of democracy. Therefore she, being a Puerto Rican, would have to belong to some
special lodge.

With all her written letters and honors attesting to her many
years of sacrifice and hard work for the chapters of this fraternal
order in Puerto Rico, the powers that be had divided her con-
cept of the brotherhood of man into white and black. She was
treated more or less like a naive old woman who had insane
notions of equality and who might eventually become another
burden to the organization because of her age.

Around this time she really started doubting the sanctity and disinterestedness of the organized church. She went to one of the best known Spanish Catholic churches and found out that you have to practically pay as you go in, just like in a movie house. This to be followed by money collections for various purposes, sometimes two or three times during the religious services.

She also found out that it was customary to hold bingo games in the church basements, and that in some of the "capillas" (chapels) without ample basement facilities, the priest just covered the saints and held dances at which "refreshments" were sold. They even had the additional convenience that these dances were never bothered by the police on superficial excuses, as were the socials held to raise the rent in the small halls of the Workers Alliance. Dancing in the church was unbelievable to her until she saw it with her own eyes.

Her thinking on this subject and the subtle changes that were taking place in her could be seen in her treatment of Father Pedro, a tall young priest who used to come to visit her when she was sick or when she took one of her long "vacations" from going to church on Sundays.

During the first year with us, Carmencita got up as soon as the Father came in and she would not sit until he did, a mark of high deference and respect among the Puerto Ricans. But after she had observed the bingo games and dances in the church, she remained seated when the priest came to visit her. She told the young priest in the most forceful and direct manner what she thought of these goings-on.

When she first came from Puerto Rico she would look cross at me when Sunday came and I chose to remain at home reading the papers. Later she did not wonder any more how a fellow like me "who did not drink, smoke or swear" could stay away from church. She even began to stay home herself, giving the excuse of her rheumatism.

Finally she developed the theory that since "Dios esta en todas partes" (God is everywhere), she might as well remain at home or go and visit a sick friend or do some other humanitarian act. Though she remained deeply religious, or more exactly, religiously dedicated to do good and to "ayudar al caido" (help the downtrodden), she rarely went to church in her later years. We could say that for the last years of her life she translated her Catholic tenets into terms of practice and tangible love and help for her fellow human beings.

The book "The Soviet Power," by the Dean of Canterbury, was published in English. We thought it would be a great idea to issue several thousand copies in Spanish. I was given the honor of publishing it in our language. This required long hours of work, far into the night.

Many a night Carmencita double checked the galleys for me, while I read the English original, before turning it over to the final proofreader.

To Carmencita the reading of "The Soviet Power" in galley form was a revelation. I remember how she used to read and reread the galleys of the chapter on Soviet women. At first she used to tell me she was rereading that chapter because she did not want any misspelled words to appear in the final copy. But in one of her unguarded moments, after once again reading the chapter on women, she placed the galleys face down on the table and exclaimed, almost inaudibly, "Unbelievable!"

It was a great emotional experience for all of us when the first half dozen copies were delivered from the binders. Carmencita pressed a book to her breast and smiled. A long, significant smile.

Then I knew that at last we were beginning to understand each other.

We never failed to tell her of the new editions of "our" book that were being issued all over Latin America. The "Soviet Power" was being serialized in dailies, weeklies, and printed by the thousands in inexpensive editions throughout the Spanish-speaking world. We told Carmencita of these and all other editions in almost every known language. She rejoiced in her nice quiet way. When we talked of more thousands of copies being printed in far off corners of the earth, she used to say as if she were meditating aloud, "It seems the world is moving."

As the Hitler hordes marched deeper and deeper inside the

Soviet Union, Carmencita got very impatient about the news of the day. I noticed that she kept on praying late into the night when the Nazis reached the outskirts of Moscow. Sometimes when I came home from meetings and assignments in the early hours of the morning, I would find her still praying. I noticed that every once in a while she would push a pin into a small cushion while she continued praying.

"What do you do that for?" I once inquired mildly.

"I do not want to lose count," she replied. "This prayer, in order to be effective, has got to be said eleven thousand times. It is called "La Oracion de las Once Mil Virgenes" (The Prayer of the Eleven Thousand Virgins).

"I started it a few months ago," she went on, "and I hope to finish it during the next few days."

"And what are you asking now with this long prayer?" I said.

I am asking the Lord that nothing will ever happen to Stalin," she answered simply and modestly.

Carmencita, I reflected, had travelled quite a bit since that day she came into our home from Puerto Rico.

29. The Lady Who Lived Near the Statue of a Man On a Horse

It was a cold January night in 1924. I was working the six to 2:30 "night shift" at the General Post Office in Brooklyn. A snow storm was raging as I stepped out on my way home a little after 2:30 that morning. As I struggled through the snow toward Tillary Street, I noticed a figure coming toward me. As it came closer to me I could distinguish a woman rather old and seemingly very tired. "Usted habla espanol?" (Do you speak Spanish?) Her voice was weak and forlorn. When I answered, "Si, hablo espanol," she breathed a deep sigh of relief. Despite the night, the snow and the wind, I could notice a hunched, weary figure becoming erect, as if a new puff of life had been injected into her.

We returned to the lobby of the Post Office where it was nice and warm. My co-workers were passing us by on their way home as I scanned the woman before me. She was dark brown; her hair was gray; her face was full of deep wrinkles. She was wearing a light summer cape not suitable at all for a wintry, snowy, January night. She had on no overshoes or rubber boots, only a pair of very worn shoes. I noticed two large holes in the soles as she took off each shoe to warm her numb cold feet with her hands. "Where do you come from?" I asked her in Spanish. "Puerto Rico." she answered.

And then, without further prompting, she told me a long story of misery and exploitation. She was a domestic worker in Puerto Rico earning a miserable monthly wage. At the house where she worked, a rich American couple came from the States to spend a few weeks there. They saw how she worked, and they liked what they saw. This couple managed to get hold of a translator through whom they proposed to the domestic worker that she come to the United States and work in their home. She accepted. Their American home was in one of the "well-to-do" parts of Brooklyn.

111

She soon found out that she had to cook, wash, iron and clean a fourteen room house full of furniture and bric-a-brac. She also found that though these two people were living in this house all by themselves they had frequent guests and gave many parties. The Puerto Rican domestic worker was supposed to clean for the numerous guests, besides cooking, washing and ironing for them while they were at the house. When the first month passed she discovered that they wanted to pay her the same miserable monthly wages she was getting from the other family in Puerto Rico!

One night, when the rich American couple had gone to sleep she packed her few belongings in the old valise that she brought from Puerto Rico and left the palatial home.

"And where did you go to?" I inquired.

"I took the first trolley car that I could find in the neighborhood, until the last stop. I left that and got into another. The main thing I wanted to do was to get as far away as possible from that house where there was all toil and no rest. At last I knocked at one door. A Negro man opened the door. He could see that I was crying and very much fatigued. He and his wife took me in. Since then, I have been living with them. One of them usually takes me to different houses to work a few hours here and a few hours there. Then one of the two, the man or his wife, comes for me during the evening.

"Yesterday morning the man took me to a house where I had worked before a few hours. I finished early. Thinking that I could get to the house all by myself, I did not wait for anybody. I thought that I took the same trolley car that they would have taken if they came for me. Somehow I did not get off where they always did. And, here I am, having taken trolley cars all day and all night, cold, hungry and tired." "And where is the house of this family with whom you are now staying?"

"All I know is that a few blocks from the house, there is a statue of a man on a horse. That is all I know."

At that late hour in the night I could think of only one solution . . . take the lady home with me. When I arrived home, I told my wife the story as briefly as possible at that late hour. She helped the woman remove all her clothing as she was cold and wet "to the bone." Then she gave her something warm to wear and some hot food to eat. Concha, my wife, was very glad that I brought the lady with me. Besides being the human thing to do, she would serve as her companion for at least a few days. We were newlyweds. Working from six to two-thirty in the morning, I left her alone every day in a four-room apartment on the top floor way out in the Williamsburg district of Brooklyn.

From then on, each Sunday early in the morning I would take our new friend with me. We spent practically all day looking for statues of men on horses. After a few Sundays we had covered almost all the squares and parks in Brooklyn, from the statue of George Washington on his horse at the Brooklyn entrance of the Williamsburg Bridge, to the most obscure statue of a man on a horse in the most remote section of every park in Brooklyn. Whenever, in our Sunday promenades I discovered a statue of a man on a horse, I pointed triumphantly to it and said: "Is that the statue?" To which, she said, at least for a half dozen Sundays, each time her voice a trifle wearier, "No, that is not the statue." Then we went home, tired and hungry and we waited for the coming Sunday hoping for better luck.

One Sunday morning about eleven o'clock we came upon a statue of a man on a horse. The lady stopped short—as soon as she saw the statue she said: "That is the one." We came upon it accidentally. The statue was in one of those places where statues have no business to be. It was on a very small Square. The man and horse seemed to be too big for the ground surrounding it. We had at last found what we were looking for these many Sundays. It seemed to me as if the statue had been waiting for us for a long time. Man and horse were so serene—not in a hurry to go anywhere. The horse's right front leg was in a graceful arched position but its hoof remained up in the air all the time we were there looking at it, never touching the ground. The left front leg never moved forward as it seemed to me the animal thing to do. But all those things were of course minor, debatable questions at that moment. The important thing was that we were looking right at THE statue the lady and myself were after for so many Sundays.

It was the statue of General Ulysses S. Grant on a horse at Bedford Avenue near Bergen Street. From this point on, the little lady seemed to know exactly where she was. She led me a few blocks to Kingston Avenue and entered an apartment building. The family was very glad and relieved to see her They had worried for weeks. They understood and were happy that she had found and would now live with people who spoke her language. She got her valise and a few of her things together and, after thanking the family very warmly—I had to translate all her phrases of gratitude and thanks—we took a taxi and came back to my home.

My wife was very pleased. She knew that my Sunday's explorations for a man on a horse were at an end.

30. Little Things Are Big

It was very late at night on the eve of Memorial Day. She came into the subway at the 34th Street Pennsylvania Station. I am still trying to remember how she managed to push herself in with a baby on her right arm, a valise in her left hand and two children, a boy and girl about three and five years old, trailing after her. She was a nice looking white lady in her early twenties.

At Nevins Street, Brooklyn, we saw her preparing to get off at the next station—Atlantic Avenue—which happened to be the place where I too had to get off. Just as it was a problem for her to get on, it was going to be a problem for her to get off the subway with two small children to be taken care of, a baby on her right arm and a medium sized valise in her left hand.

And there I was, also preparing to get off at Atlantic Avenue, with no bundles to take care of—not even the customary book under my arm without which I feel that I am not completely dressed.

As the train was entering the Atlantic Avenue station, some white man stood up from his seat and helped her out, placing the children on the long, deserted platform. There were only two adult persons on the long platform some time after midnight on the eve of last Memorial Day.

I could perceive the steep, long concrete stairs going down to the Long Island Railroad or into the street. Should I offer my help as the American white man did at the subway door placing the two children outside the subway car? Should I take care of the girl and the boy, take them by their hands until they reached the end of the steep long concrete stairs of the Atlantic Avenue station.

Courtesy is a characteristic of the Puerto Rican. And here I was—a Puerto Rican—hours past midnight, a valise, two white

115

children and a white lady with a baby on her arm palpably need-ing somebody to help her at least until she descended the long concrete stairs.

But how could I, a Negro and a Puerto Rican approach this white lady who very likely might have preconceived prejudices against Negroes and everybody with foreign accents, in a deserted subway station very late at night?

What would she say? What would be the first reaction of this white American woman, perhaps coming from a small town with a valise, two children and a baby on her right arm? Would she say: Yes, of course, you may help me. Or would she think that I was just trying to get too familiar? Or would she think worse than that perhaps? What would I do if she let out a scream as I went toward her to offer my help?

Was I misjudging her? So many slanders are written every day in the daily press against the Negroes and Puerto Ricans. I hesitated for a long, long minute. The ancestral manners that the most illiterate Puerto Rican passes on from father to son were strug-gling inside me. Here was I, way past midnight, face to face with a situation that could very well explode into an outburst of prejudices and chauvinistic conditioning of the "divide and rule" policy of present day society.

It was a long minute. I passed on by her as if I saw nothing. As if I was insensitive to her need. Like a rude animal walking on two legs, I just moved on half running by the long subway platform leaving the children and the valise and her with the baby on her arm. I took the steps of the long concrete stairs in twos until I reached the street above and the cold air slapped my warm face.

This is what racism and prejudice and chauvinism and official artificial divisions can do to people and to a nation!

Perhaps the lady was not prejudiced after all. Or not preju-diced enough to scream at the coming of a Negro toward her in a solitary subway station a few hours past midnight.

If you were not that prejudiced, I failed you, dear lady. I know that there is a chance in a million that you will read these lines. I am willing to take that millionth chance. If you were not that prejudiced, I failed you, lady, I failed you, children. I failed myself to myself.

I buried my courtesy early on Memorial Day morning. But here is a promise that I make to myself here and now; if I am ever faced with an occasion like that again, I am going to offer my help regardless of how the offer is going to be received.

Then I will have my courtesy with me again.

31. The Mother, the Young Daughter, Myself and All of Us

I was drinking a cup of coffee in one of those new places where the counter is built in a zig-zag way, like a curving long line of conga dancers. The high stools follow the wavy contours of the counter, making little bays of tall seats where the patrons seat themselves placing their feet in a sort of iron stirrup.

That day every stool was taken but one, on my right side, and another, three stools further to my left.

A mother and her young daughter about nine years old, came in evidently to have a snack.

"You sit by the gentleman," meaning me . . . the mother said to her young daughter pointing to the unoccupied stool on my right. "I will be sitting over there," the mother added, pointing to the other empty stool three seats to my left.

"I won't sit beside no nigger," said the child.

And the mother, myself, and all of us never said a word.

32. Greetings From Washington

John and his wife Mary went to Washington on his vacation to see the cherry blossoms, and to see Washington. John and I are good friends though we think very differently. John thinks it is too bad that "a man like you" should have such "crazy ideas!" John has one very good quality. He has a sense of humor. John also likes to tease.

So while in Washington, he sent me a postcard, with a picture of the Lincoln Memorial on it. In the writing space of the card he wrote: "Greetings from Washington! City of democracy, equality and freedom! Having a wonderful time—John and Mary." I would not doubt that perhaps John and Mary were having a wonderful time. They are white. And they had vacation money systematically put aside every week of the year for just such an occasion.

So anything can happen in Washington, D. C., capital of the United States of America. If you are white and have a little money to spend. You might even be happy if you are the kind of a person who doesn't look too closely and ask too many questions; if you are more or less insensitive to what happens to others and how the other half lives. You might even be happy in Washington, D. C.

When I said that anything can happen in Washington, I am not referring to what is taking place inside the Pentagon or in the White House, important as those things are for all of us. I am referring to everyday happenings in the lives of ordinary citizens, especially those not of the white race who go out to the U. S. Capital.

In Washington I have seen a man break the glass in which he has served an orange refreshment to a Negro, in front of him right after the Negro had finished drinking from the glass. I have seen in Washington . . . But what is the use. There are so many instances of race discrimination in Washington against colored diplomats, artists, scientists and ordinary laymen that just to enumerate them will take hundreds of pages, from Marian Anderson to the end of the alphabet.

One time I went to Washington. I don't remember on what delegation or committee. It would take us at least two days to finish our business in the Capital. So I took every precaution to see that I had a place to sleep at least for a night. A friend gave me a letter to a Negro family in Washington. They would have space for me to sleep for one night. The delegation went to the various offices we had to go to. After a good day's legwork from building to building we went into one of the government cafeterias —one of the few places where Negroes and whites can eat together unmolested—in downtown Washington—and had our supper. We agreed on a place in which we were to meet next morning and everybody left for the house in which a nice soft bed was waiting for him. Or so I thought.

I went to the Negro family's address to whom our mutual friend in New York had given me a very nice letter of introduction. I knocked on the door and waited. After a while, I knocked again. Then again and more persistently and strongly. A neighbor in the next apartment opened the door. "Are you looking for Mr. and Mrs.——" "Yes." "They went to New York for a few days to visit their folks in Jamaica, Long Island."

"What shall I do now?" I thought to myself. It was already around 8:30 or 9:00 o'clock in the evening. I had a little over twenty dollars in my wallet. I went to the railroad station and returned the little overnight valise to one of the boxes in which, for twenty-five cents, you could lock anything from a briefcase to a suitcase. I wanted to be free to walk and move around without any extra weight bothering me. Then I started to look for a place to sleep.

I visited half a dozen hotels large and medium size. They all said the same thing: No colored people allowed. When I went to three or four rather dilapidated and suspicious looking rooming houses offering any price they asked for a cot somewhere in which to pass the night, I met with the same answer: "No colored allowed."

Suddenly I remembered that a Jewish friend had given me the telephone of a girl friend of his who worked for the government in Washington. I had it written on the margin of my *New York Times* that I had in the valise and that I had no time to read during the day. I went back to the railroad station to get the valise and the address.

By now it was eleven o'clock at night. I called the number, gave my friend's name in New York, as an introduction. Then I explained my situation. Everything. She told me to come but not to take the elevator. She explained that she lived in an apartment building for whites only. If anybody knew that she was inviting a Negro to sleep at her place, she would be sure to lose her apartment— So she gave me her apartment number and detailed instructions on how to avoid being seen coming in by anybody. I will remember that night all my life. I went into that apartment building as if I were actually going to commit a crime. Avoiding everybody, walking on tip toes as silently and stealthily as possible! And to think that I was going to do what millions of people were doing in over half the world at that very hour: Going to sleep! But in Washington the "Capital of the world's greatest democracy," I had to act like a thief just to get a place where I could go to bed and fall asleep!

The young lady shared the apartment with another office worker friend of hers. I slept on a sofa in the parlor. It was agreed that I would get up very early so that I could leave as unseen as I came in the night before. This I did. All this happened a few years ago. If you place the two young ladies—they must be older now—right in front of me today, I confess that I would not recognize them. All I know is that both of them were waiting for my knock, dressed in their housecoats, when I came into their apartment. Wherever you are ladies, from these pages of reminiscences, thank you again.

But the most tragic figures are those Washington visitors who think that the White House, and the Capitol, the Senators and Congressmen are just oozing democracy and justice from every

pore of their bodies. They pretend to be very frank and very open
—all hail fellows, well met, all around. These visitors who usually
go on delegations to the Capital get the education of their lives
in just one day of delegation work in Washington. That is if they
go on one of those delegations that are demanding something not
exactly to the liking of the esteemed Senators and Congressmen.
The young enthusiasts who had read of the Jackson and Lincoln
periods in the presidency—these young people as they go to a
Senator's or Congressman's spacious office with their demands
and their signed petitions and when they think they are going to
be received by the representative himself, in person, they are
received by the secretary to the third secretary of the most honorable representative. It is advisable that at that moment of
awakening to reality, someone who has gone through that experience before be there with the new ones. That will be just the
time to tell them what the score is and the importance of going back
to their respective states and cities to see that Senators and
Congressmen, like the late Vito Marcantonio, for example, be sent
to Washington. If there is a good teacher to show them the
political facts of life at that very moment of the cold formal
reception from the secretary to the third secretary of the legislator
that they helped send to Washington, that could be perhaps the
turning point in their political way of thinking.

I remember the time that Ava Miranda and some of her friends
went from Brooklyn to visit their uncle in Washington. Some of
the girls were white and some were Negroes. Their uncle, a
Puerto Rican veteran of the first world war, had lived in Washington for many years. He was supposed to be a "small" big
shot in Washington. A Puerto Rican who felt himself to be 200
per cent American, who on Armistice Day was the first to be in
line with his 1917 uniform, ribbons, and medals, ready to parade
down Pennsylvania Avenue and show the world the equality,
freedom and liberty you could find in Washington, Capital of
the U.S.A. He was the kind who believed in everything that the
books said—and then more. He was a Puerto Rican who had
gradually and unconsciously converted himself into a flag waving,
pledge taking, bigger and better 200 per cent American.

As soon as the girls left the New York train, uncle took them to the first restaurant in sight. The restaurant owner insisted he would serve the white girls but not the Negro girls. Uncle was very much incensed. He felt it was his obligation to prove to the young ladies that there was equality and democracy in Washington. "I am a veteran of the First World War. Remember THAT!" he used to shout when somebody dared to doubt that he would be able to do anything about it. When they were not served at the restaurant, uncle went to the Police Department. He went to the higher authorities. There he was courteously laughed at. He made dozens of telephone calls and kept writing dozens of letters long after the young ladies returned to New York. Yes, sir, he wanted to prove to the girls that there was such a thing as equality and democracy in Washington. I heard uncle died without even being able to win an apology from the restaurant owners.

As we wrote at the beginning, there are thousands of cases to prove that even with all the late attempts to reform the reactionary racists, the government servants and the general owning class in Washington, it will be years before a particle of racial equality and democratic treatment for any non-white coming to Washington from any part of the world would be put into practice.

Take the case of the Puerto Rican school teachers invited to Washington at the end of the school year in Puerto Rico. When the Puerto Rican teachers got to Washington, they were divided according to their color. The whites were housed in downtown hotels, the Negroes or those appearing to be Negroes were sent to dormitories in Howard University or in the neighborhood of that famous Negro institution of learning.

Or take the case of Rosa and Maria, her daughter. When a Puerto Rican family in Harlem told me how Rosa, an old friend of mine, visited Maria, her only daughter, working in Washington, every other week-end; I was not amazed as much as the Harlem Puerto Rican family I was visiting. I told them that those "happenings" were common in Washington, the "great democratic Capital of the United States," to use John's phrase on his Lincoln Memorial greeting card.

This is the story as the family told it to me. Maria answered a federal application for Spanish-English stenographer in Washington. We all knew that Maria was a very bright kid. A very good office worker and secretary. Maria was living with a white family in Washington. All her friends were white Americans. She was actually "passing" as white. Rosa, her mother would not pass for anything but a Negro. Rosa's husband, Maria's father, who died when Maria was still a child, was white. This is a very familiar man-woman—or vice versa—marriage relationship in Puerto Rico.

So when Rosa went to "visit" her daughter every other week end, Maria waited for her at the Washington train station. They walked on the streets and avenues near the train station. Maria usually had some home-made sandwiches. They ate them at some public park. Maria would not risk the possibility of going into one of the government cafeterias and finding one of her acquaintances. After the sandwiches, they walked and talked some more until the six o'clock train was about to leave for New York, Maria gave a formal train kiss to her mother and they said goodbye until two Saturdays hence.

I suppose that some Saturday, Rosa and Maria felt adventurous enough to get away from the railroad station surroundings and walk as far as the Lincoln Memorial. I imagine them there admiring the great statue of Abraham Lincoln, sitting in his imposing marble armchair high up there upon its marble pedestal in the very central point of interest of the imposing structure. I imagine Rosa and Maria being held spellbound by that modest and humble figure of Lincoln and by all the humane things he stood for. And as Rosa and Maria were preparing to leave the Lincoln Memorial they would pause a minute to listen to a child holding his father's hand and reading haltingly from the south wall of the Memorial:

FOUR SCORE AND SEVEN YEARS AGO
OUR FATHERS BROUGHT FORTH ON THIS CONTINENT
A NEW NATION, CONCEIVED IN LIBERTY
AND DEDICATED TO THE PROPOSITION THAT

ALL MEN ARE CREATED EQUAL.

I could imagine, after listening to that phrase for the ages, mother and daughter walking back in silence to the railroad station. And the daughter saying, as the train eased its way out: "I'll see you in two weeks." And the mother answering meditatively: "Yes."

Greetings from Washington!

33. Because He Spoke in Spanish

It was past midnight when Bernabe Nunez and his brother Wilfredo, entered a bar in the Williamsburg section of Brooklyn. Bernabe was in a happy mood. He had recently been discharged from the army after serving in Korea. His father, Francisco Nunez, was in good health in his hometown of Lares, Puerto Rico. Bernabe's wife was expecting in Stanton, California, from where Bernabe was planning to bring her to Brooklyn. He had just found a job.

So Bernabe had all the reasons in the world to find himself in a happy mood.

There was still one ambition he had not realized. To have his first subway ride. This was a childhood ambition he had promised himself. If he ever went to New York, first thing he would do would be to take a subway ride.

Spanish is the language of the Puerto Rican nation. Bernabe was proud of being a Puerto Rican. He also recognized the great civil, political and human rights embodied in the Declaration of Independence and the Constitution of the United States. I am afraid that Bernabe did not know that the rights written in the Declaration and in the Constitution have some greater potential rights and freedoms implicit in them. That these rights are maturing in the minds of the people. I am almost sure that Bernabe Nunez and his brother Wilfredo did not know about a thing called qualitative change. I doubt whether it is important that Bernabe knew this scientific term as long as this change continues relentlessly day by day, second by second, counting the few years of life left to the system that is the source of all evil—capitalism.

Bernabe Nunez and his brother knew that there is at least enough democracy in New York to go into a bar and have a couple of beers celebrating his release from the army. As they

126

were peacefully drinking their beer at the bar, Bernabe and Wilfredo went to try their luck at the slot machines. A dozen young men started to circulate among the other persons trying to procure their silent approval of what they were about to do.

Wilfredo went to the men's room for a few minutes. When he came out, his brother Bernabe was not in the bar. The dozen young thugs that had objected to the brothers speaking in Spanish had disappeared. As Wilfredo came out of the bar, he saw his brother lying on the sidewalk, and the thugs booting Bernabe. Wilfredo was also beaten. Bernabe's head and ribs were fractured, his face was a mess of blood, and his stomach was ripped open. He was kicked to death.

Thousands of Puerto Ricans went to the funeral parlor where Bernabe's body was laid. Many more thousands from all over the city went to the special mass at the Miraculous Virgin Church on 114th Street on the corner of St. Nicholas Avenue, in Harlem. The cold murder of Bernabe Nunez was the only conversational theme in Puerto Rican and other Latin American homes for many days.

We are not against committees of "respectable citizens" seeing the Mayor about our civil rights and liberties. We don't oppose editorials in the Spanish press in which Commissioner of Police Stephen P. Kennedy° is very cavalierly taken to task, about the deficiencies of his police department, in guarding the citizens' safety and the out and out discrimination and third degree methods applied against the Negroes and the Puerto Ricans in his police precincts. We are not opposed, of course, to a leaflet being mimeographed and distributed.

But it seems to us that there is something more to be done. Much more. And that is the day to day organization of the Puerto Rican and American communities for action, led by progressives and the many other democracy-loving Puerto Ricans and North Americans—Negro and white—lest another Bernabe Nunez is murdered by the loud minority of racist and reactionary

° This essay was written before Police Commissioner Kennedy resigned on February 24, 1961.

thinking persons that unfortunately exist in every community.

Let us join the Tenants Councils, the political clubs, the Community Center, the PTA, and the fraternal and religious organizations, according to our beliefs. And in all those institutions, let us think and act like progressives—humbly, modestly, but actively progressive. Let us permeate our neighborhoods—our city and state —with progressive thinking, progressive literature, progressive action.

Let us not be silent wherever we are, and wherever our voice or our written word is needed for the defense of a just cause. We are sure that if only one decent American would have firmly spoken that night at the bar, when Bernabe was murdered, the hands of the young thugs would perhaps have been stopped.

We are not going to give you here a one-two-three quickie program against discrimination and for civil rights. This is not the appropriate page for that. This will surely be done somewhere else.

What we are saying now is that in order to avoid future murders and violations of rights, we have to organize the broad forces of decency in the neighborhoods for simple democratic rights. Out of the practice of simple democracy, a higher and deeper understanding of the principle will come.

And then . . .

But I am not going to use the phrase "qualitative change," again in this column today. I just will not.

34. Youth: The Palisades as a Backdrop

I was very tired. I felt I needed at least three days away from the city noises and the telephone. So I convinced Concha that she should accompany me to one of the workers' camps to spend the weekend.

We arrived Friday evening just in time to listen to the last announcement over the public address system informing everybody that there was to be a campfire at the edge of the cliff fronting the Hudson River that very night.

After arranging for accommodations, my wife and I started to walk single file leaving all the camp's cabins far behind. We passed bushes and walked through lanes of nature's little gems, beauty bathed in sweet calmness. The crickets provided the musical background, dissonance that you somehow found to your liking. Concha kept back of me. My flashlight told her where to step next.

Now we heard the singing and the guitars like a long lost echo repeated by the trees that extended tall and erect, dissimilar in size like the pipes of a monumental organ. Now we could see the reflection of the campfire bursting the compact darkness of the night with its glare.

At last we got there. Twenty or thirty teenagers with a sprinkling of middle-aged and old—both sexes and of various colors—sprawled around a campfire that was growing as the young people threw more pieces of dry wood into it.

In the middle of the group stood a Negro woman. I was told later that she was in her fifties. But there, that night, gleaming all over with the reflection of the fire on her lithe, sylph-like body, she looked as young as any of the teenagers. Concha, my wife, said: "She looks like a goddess." "Goddess? There are no such things as goddesses. These are only imaginary things from the

129

pages of old books on Greece and Rome," I objected mildly, showing off a little of my erudition. Concha just responded to my professional answer by reflecting a little more affirmatively: "She looks like a goddess."

"But did you hear what I was saying? That goddesses are imaginary creations in Greek and Roman . . ." Concha interrupted me and repeated again this time pointing to her. "She looks like a goddess." I thought I could clinch this little argument with a brutal knock-down-drag-out unanswerable question: "Have you ever seen a goddess?" Concha's answers came in rapidly. "No, but still I say: 'She looks like a goddess!'" The firmness of conviction in Concha's voice made me examine the Negro woman's silhouette standing like a glint of light in the middle of the group around the campfire. And I had to admit that she looked like a goddess though I conceded that I had never seen a goddess myself.

We started to squeeze in unobtrusively and easily until we made ourselves part of the circle.

The youth sang individually and in chorus. The guitars were right there, keeping pace with the voices. The voices spoke—the guitars answered. On the other side of the river like an immense theatre backdrop were the Palisades and the Hudson River. The Palisades have seen Henry Hudson in his "Half Moon" following up the stream in his hopeless search for a passage to India. But the Palisades had never before seen a campfire like the one that night.

Youth with its enthusiasm saw to it that neither the fire nor the singing would die out. Concha and I sat there looking and listening. The hours passed by and nobody cared where the hours went. It was a wonderful night all around.

The bell for the morning breakfast rang three times. The stomach insisted that we get up. Unwillingly we obeyed. During breakfast the program for the morning was announced. Those who were practicing for the Saturday night show, were asked to the open theatre at the clearing near the river.

We strolled around the grounds, visiting familiar spots that we knew from previous trips to the camp. The social hall and theatre, the canteen (meeting place between meals, just before

you go into the lake). We kept on exploring until we came to
the open theatre.

There on the wooden platform about a dozen teenagers were
reciting in unison the famous poem by Emma Lazarus:

> *Give me your tired, your poor,*
> *Your huddled masses yearning to breathe free,*
> *The wretched refuse of your teeming shore.*
> *Send these, the homeless, tempest-tossed to me,*
> *I lift my lamp beside the golden door!*

Again the Negro woman was in front leading them, teaching
them, the recitation of that inspiring poem.

She directed them like a symphony orchestra. Every accent
badly stressed was corrected. Every exaggerated gesture was
lovingly subdued. Somebody told us she was not only a great
teacher, but a great poetess and actress. It was a delight to see
those youths responding with feeling and imagination to the
instructions of the tall, slim Negro woman.

The whole scene looked to me like a page out of the future.

35. And Fuchik Looked On Confident

The federal agents came to take over our paper. They swooped down on us by surprise as if we might run away with the old empty safe or the broken down addressograph machine.

Hiding the real motives under the pretext that the paper owed some taxes to the government, they came to suppress one of the clearest dissenting voices in the country against the shame of discrimination, exploitation and brink diplomacy.

I don't remember exactly how many they were. They were a flock of tall, self-assured young men displaying that artificial courtesy that is shown by those who feel they have the power—though not the glory.

These young men were just the instruments through which suppression of free speech and free press was being placed in operation. I wonder what they will be telling their grandchildren about their day of invasion of the *Daily Worker* 20 years from now.

I would have loved to be present at the pep talk administered by their chief before they came to the *Daily Worker* on the pretext of collecting unpaid taxes. After the pep talk by their chief the young men of course must have felt very patriotic and they swooped into our paper ready to encounter the enemy

> *Theirs not to make reply,*
> *Theirs not to reason why*
> *Theirs but to do and die.*

They came into the large room where I work and started to look importantly around pasting notices of "WARNING" on every door, a warning reading that from that moment on, the whole office was seized by the Treasury authorities.

As they moved around with an air of futile efficiency, I noticed a picture that has been hanging on the wall of that room for many years. A picture on the wall above an old desk that nobody uses. It is the picture of a man in his late thirties with a stack of black unruly hair above his forehead. He looked strong, smiling and confident.

It is the picture of Julius Fuchik, the writer, people's leader and national hero of today's free and democratic Czechoslovakia. Fuchik was murdered by the Nazi beasts on September 8, 1943 after years of persecution, inhuman tortures in fascist dungeons and concentration camps.

It seems to me as if Julius Fuchik was taking it all with a smile from his picture on the wall. And as the government agents continued to look back of every desk and into every nook and corner of the paper Fuchik seemed to be telling me from his picture on the wall: "Jesus, it has all been done before. It has all been tried before. Remember?"

And as I recalled how the fascists of Italy and Germany and their henchmen in other countries tried to destroy the press and enslave the people, I remembered one sentence from Fuchik's unforgettable *Notes from the Gallows*:

"Oh what a crop will rise one day from that frightful seeding."

And as the federal agents continued their own comings and goings trying in their futile efficiency to impress us with their ersatz importance, I kept looking at Julius Fuchik up there on the wall, so serene, so handsome, so confident, his eyes so full of the future and of triumph. I smiled back at him. And I became suddenly ever more confident of the final victory of the working class and its progressive peace-loving allies in all other sectors of society.

The City Room was full of cameras, photographers and writers from the various national and international news services. The *Daily Worker* staff continued the daily task of producing the most honest daily paper in America.

The seizure of the paper has been quite an experience for all of us. I hope it will be a real lesson for the whole country and a great reminder that even in these post-Geneva days the forces of McCarthyism are not altogether dead. The seizure of the paper should be a lesson for those who have been sitting on an ideological fence for years telling themselves that things like the closing of daily papers could not happen in this country.

That evening I left the *Daily Worker* building feeling that somehow, somewhere the paper was going to come out the next day and every day as it has been coming out for the last 32 years.

And as I was about to leave, I went over to Fuchik's picture and said to him: "Hasta Manana." And I slowly read for the nth time the famous words in his last will which were printed under the picture.

"We live for happiness. For that we went to battle, for that we die. Let grief never be connected with our name."

36. Wanted — A Statue

We cannot really tell you how many statues there are in New York City. We do not know when they were last counted by the Park Department. We are sure—very sure—that among all the statues in the city, from those of John Ercikson and Giuseppe Garibaldi: at the Battery Park to those of Heinrich Heine and Louis J. Heintz in the Bronx, there is not one statue of a Puerto Rican in all the marble and bronze figures in the city.

But someone may ask: why do the Puerto Ricans or, for that matter, any nationality need a statue? Well, we might answer that statues serve as inspiration; as historical reminders of a healthful pride in one's people's contributions to the collective cultural heritage of humanity. We might also add that statues have also many more useful and prosaic purposes. They are decorations and markers for the cities. They serve as a place for birds to build their nests and chirp and warble their loves.

They are very lofty altitudes from which pigeons can, in all immunity, bombard our egos with the excess baggage on their bodies, while we are seriously bent on reading the inscription at the pedestal. Statues serve as a place to rest and meditate for a while after a long trek of job hunting through the streets of the immense city.

But of course, the most important purpose of a statue is to remind us that in every people there exist the spark and inspiration to do and to produce great deeds and great works to be added to the greatness of humankind.

There is hardly a nation that is not represented in the various statues that decorate parks, museums, libraries, streets and avenues of this city. Every nationality save the Puerto Ricans has a statue.

We are not proposing a long list of names or projecting our own candidate for a statue of a Puerto Rican in New York. We

135

do believe, however, that ways and means should be found to set up a statue of a Puerto Rican—man or woman—somewhere in the midst of this city that over 600,000 Puerto Ricans have chosen to call their home.

Other nationalities have their own statues. There is one of Giovanni da Verrazano at Battery Park, built by popular contributions sent to an Italian newspaper in the city. There's the statue of Edward Grieg, the Norwegian composer, in the Flower Garden at Prospect Park, presented in 1914 to the city of New York by the Norwegian Societies of this city. There are the statues of Simon Bolivar and Jose de San Martin at 59th Street and the Avenue of Americas, both presented to New York City. The first was presented by Venezuela and the second by the city of Buenos Aires in Argentina.

One thing we should be against from the start. If the Puerto Ricans are going to have their statue, let us see to it that it will not be placed somewhere in Puerto Rican Harlem where only the Puerto Ricans will pass by and notice it. We want this Puerto Rican to be in the very heart of the city. Say, somewhere in the Avenue of the Americas, on 41st Street, thus giving a correct decorative balance to that side of Bryant Park that now has at its 42nd Street entrance the statue of Jose Bonifacio de Andrada e Silva, the great patriarch of Brazilian independence.

Some years ago, when we first thought of this idea and when we had some progressive councilmen in the City Council, we were many times tempted to write to them and outline our plan. We even had a sketch for the plaza at 110 Street and Fifth Avenue. We proposed that this circle on the north eastern entrance to Central Park be called Hostos Square. A statue of Eugenio Maria de Hostos to be placed in the very middle of it.

But as the years passed, we came to realize that Hostos is not of the Puerto Ricans alone but of all the Americas and the whole world. Such a statue should be in the heart of the greatest city in the world.

And here am I breaking my vow not to project any candidates!

Just as the other nationalities have statues where they go to place flower offerings on their national holidays, we Puerto Ricans

would like to have a marble symbol as hard as the lives we live
here, but as full of beauty and dignity as the life that we are
building together with the rest of our brother New Yorkers for a
future of freedom and abundance for all.

37. The Library Looks at the Puerto Ricans

If you drop into any of the branch public libraries in Manhattan you can get, for free, a list of books dealing with Puerto Rico and the Puerto Ricans living in New York. The whole Branch Library Book News for the month of February, 1956 is dedicated to Puerto Ricans.

Though we don't have to tell you that most of the books recommended are not written in a favorable light, this shows at least a recognition that the Puerto Rican carries weight today and that the Puerto Rican is here to stay.

The publication of this list goes to show you, moreover, that the Puerto Ricans are growing in importance. The library is telling the people of New York that we are a nation with our own territory, our own economy, language and culture.

In its book news for February, the New York Public Library gives a list of books in English and another in Spanish about Puerto Rico and the Puerto Ricans. The Spanish list is divided into sections: novels and short stories, poets and poems, the theatre, folklore, about people, history, miscellany. The list of the books in English is also divided into sections: Presenting Puerto Rico, of poets and music, our New York neighbors, children's books.

If we consider that ninety-five percent of the Puerto Ricans living in New York are workers, a section of Puerto Rican books and pamphlets dealing with trade unions and Puerto Rican labor in general would have been very much in order.

Another section that we consider should have been included is one dealing with the activities and exhibitions put on by Puerto Rican and American librarians in many of the branch libraries. Special mention should have been given to the Aguilar Library at 110th Street near Third Avenue, where many activities especially geared to the Puerto Rican in the neighborhood have been going on for years, and where files of important newspapers and maga-

zine articles about Puerto Rico and the Puerto Ricans here are
kept for consultation by the general public.

Speaking of clippings of important newspaper series and articles
on Puerto Rico, it is regrettable that a section of the Branch Library
Book News for February did not point out the series of articles
on Puerto Rico that have appeared in our metropolitan dailies,
weeklies and monthly magazines. We don't have to emphasize
that the reader has to be extremely careful in reading all these
articles, in order to be able to separate the positive from the nega-
tive and chauvinistic in the material presented.

It seems to us that, where the library really does not do credit
to itself is in its failure to publicize the numerous rare books and
material on Puerto Rico that it has on its shelves and in its vaults.
We refer to such books as the "Historia Geografica, Civil y Natural
de la Isla de San Juan Bautista de Puerto Rico"—Geographic,
Civil and Natural History of Puerto Rico—written by Inigo Abad
Lasierra and printed in Madrid, Spain in 1782. This book is in
the manuscript division of the Library and is a book of inestimable
value and primary material on the historical and cultural development of Puerto Rico.

Another section that we should like to have seen included
in the list is one on reference books on Puerto Rico. We don't
see why "El Libro de Puerto Rico"—The Book of Puerto Rico—
written both in English and Spanish and which I have consulted
many times at the main library, was not included in the list.
Though printed in 1923, it is still a great source book, especially
for those who lack the knowledge of the Spanish language.

Other reference material that should have been mentioned is
the *Encyclopedia Espana,* which includes in its more than eighty
volumes, plenty of material about Puerto Rico and many biographical sketches of Puerto Ricans, like Betances and Hostos, to
which the *Encyclopedia Britannica* does not give even one line.
The *Espana* is one of the great world encyclopedias. In some
future time a Republican Spain will make of the *Espana* an even
greater reference work than it is today.

If the Committee entrusted with the compilation of the book
list on Puerto Rico would have gone deeper in searching the

very same library archives of 42nd Street, they would have come across the September 4, 1948 issue of "Puerto Rico Illustrado," one of the Puerto Rican magazines kept in its collection, in which Jose Ferrer (not the actor but a Puerto Rican writer and university professor) compiled a list of ALL the books on Puerto Rico with their call number in that library. This work was entrusted to Professor Ferrer by the Cervantes Fraternal Society of the International Workers Order. They could have avoided many hours of research and work by just reading the article in "Puerto Rico Illustrado." (Readers of this column know that the Cervantes Fraternal Society of the I.W.O. with its Puerto Rican People's Chorus, its children's dancing ensembles and other cultural activities, together with other national societies of the I.W.O. were the victims of fascist persecution and McCarthyite destruction in cold war America.)

We also missed in the branch library news for February dedicated to Puerto Rico, any mention of the Schomburg Collection, at 135th Street and Lenox Avenue. Though the collection itself is dedicated to the Negro people and their history, there is a great amount of material on prominent Negro Puerto Ricans in its files. Besides, Arturo Schomburg, a great figure in the life of the 19th century Puerto Rican in New York was himself a Puerto Rican, born in San Juan, the capital of Puerto Rico.

It seems to me that one of the main divisions in the New York Public Library system—bearing the name of a great Negro Puerto Rican should at least have been mentioned in a library publication purporting to compile the most important books dealing with the cultural developments and contributions of Puerto Rico and the Puerto Ricans in New York.

38. On Singing in the Shower

Just as there are people who love to read in the bathtub, there are people who like to sing in the shower. They take their bathing standing up.

Singing in the shower is not like singing in a parlor or on the stage. In order to be asked to sing in a parlor you must have a certain amount of talent. You are asked to sing because somebody has heard you before in some other parlor. To sing in the shower is not like chanting on the stage. On the stage you have to be a singer. Under the shower you don't even have to be. You just sing ... or you think you do. Besides, you don't get paid for singing under the vertical water of the shower. Shower singing is akin to that done under the balcony of a beautiful senorita on a tropical night with a full moon and a million stars lit up there just for you and your love, intently listening from the back of the latticed window. You must love to sing, in order to do it in the shower. That does not mean of course that because you love it you must know how to sing. Those are two different things altogether. Just like in serenading. Because you love to sing to your Juliet it does not follow that you can crow to the mysteries of the musical scale.

In fact, there are some lovers who hire singers and players to convey for them in musical tremolos the love they feel deep in whatever place love is supposed to be felt. We have heard of lovers who have brought victrolas with them to serenade their sweathearts for better or worse—perhaps for worse. And perhaps you read about the Romeo who hired a truck, placed a piano and pianist in it and ordered the player to play underneath the balcony of his beloved.

But of course, you cannot think of bringing a piano, not to mention a pianist or a singer, into the shower room to play for you or sing while you bathe.

That is why singing in the shower is strictly a do-it-yourself job. And as in every other field, you have good, bad and indifferent. You have the fellow who chants in the church choir. He twitters high and solemnly in the shower. He is more inclined to slow music like hymns and old ballads. He takes his time to give forth every note while moving the cake of soap over the whole surface of his body at a sort of funeral-march pace.

But sometimes even this type of singer gets a little livelier and faster in his singing. All of a sudden he is inspired and he starts humming with his head pointing towards the ceiling and he lets go with all the air in his lungs and all the faith in his heart as if any minute he will see Gabriel's trumpet piercing the bathroom ceiling announcing the coming of the Lord. And while you are outside waiting in line, changing from one foot to the other he will be lustily caroling:

> *Mine eyes have seen the glory*
> *Of the coming of the Lord*
> *He hath trampled out the vintage*
> *Where the grapes of wrath are stored . . .*

When this happens, you'd better cede your place in line in front of the bathroom to anybody who wants it . . . for he will stay, trilling his hymns almost to the very minute when he thinks that Christ will be coming to visit the earth for the second time—and that, if you ask me, means a lot of waiting.

In progressive homes you get the singer in the shower who loves labor and revolutionary songs. By the songs they sing, you can more or less tell how many years they have been in the movement. If he gives forth with: "Far and wide as the eyes can wander" . . . you know he is an oldtimer.

Then you have the singer without a song. While the water is beating away at his body, he starts thinking of what he should sing to enjoy his bath the more. He goes into "Cielito Lindo," and then realizes that he does not know all the music or all the words—so he shifts to: "Let me call you sweetheart." He feels waltzy for a while—sometimes with disastrous consequences. But he drops that after coming to the conclusion that he only knows the popular refrain that gives its name to the waltz. After running through it two or three times . . . "Let me call you sweetheart . . . la, la, la, la, la," he gives up and settles for the la la la la la part which is a lyric quite universal with those who do not know how to sing.

Singing in the shower is not like singing or whistling while passing a cemetery on a pitch black night. If you are superstitious you may work yourself into the certainty that somebody is harmonizing alongside of you while humming past a cemetery.

Shower singing serves a purpose. It expands your lungs. It not only helps to reveal the time you came into the progressive movement but it aids in the discovery of your age. For example if you start with:

> *There are smiles*
> *That make us happy*
> *There are smiles*
> *That make us blue . . .*

You can surmise that the person rejoicing in that song under the pressure of the shower was a teenager around the year 1925.

Singing in the shower is more like humming in the subway. You compete with the noise of the water splashing its silver on the bottom of the bathtub as you compete with the noise of the subway wheels as they pick up speed from one express station to the other. But only up to here you can compare singing in the subway with singing under the shower. For in the subway you are all dressed, and surrounded with people on all sides, thinking of the nice cold shower you are going to take as soon as you get home.

There are people who love to sing marches and arias full of festive spirit, while they are taking a shower. They use their breast as a sort of drum and the cake of soap as a drum stick to beat out the la la la la, stamping in the tub to the time of the "1812 Overture," thinking perhaps that they are in hot pursuit of Napoleon through the muddy white-gray snow banks of old Russia. They seem to get a kick out of it. Sometimes they smile as if saying to themselves— "What fools we mortals be," or words to that effect. And then they go into sonorous laughter that pours spontaneously from their throats without logical rhyme or reason. That is the time that the wife on the outside impatiently cries: "Are you crazy?" While he answers from the inside: "Yes!" And the water from the shower keeps rolling along. And the laughter grows in volume and momentum after that. Sometimes a long silence supersedes the singing. That is the time he has dropped the cake . . . and with soap in his eyes and ears, he tries to catch the slippery bar of soap on the bottom of the tub as if playing blind man's buff with it.

In this singing under the shower there is a growing fraternity of people who recite instead. You could listen to them all over the place while they go through the whole of . . . "Friends, Romans, countrymen, lend me your ears . . ." as if they were saying it from the old Roman forum—or they might go into Poe's "The Bells" . . . and the bells, bells, bells, bells, bells, bells—are heard in such an enthusiastic and repetitive manner that when by sheer exhaustion they finish repeating the darn words, they usually wind up with more bells than we have in all of the churches in New York. Sometimes, in their enthusiasm and lyric drunkeness, they keep on saying bells, bells, bells with the face receiving the whole force of the shower and the mouth fills with water until it overflows onto the chin and chest. Then all of Poe's poetry converts itself into a lyric gargle which is a pity, but a relief to the ones who have been waiting outside for hours.

There is also a lusty group who rehearse the "just a few words" they were asked to say at some place in honor of something or other, while they take that all-important quick shower before they present themselves before the public, dressed in their installment-plan best.

Sometimes you are lucky enough to participate in what might be properly called a collective shower. Like when you are vacationing in one of the workers' camps. Before supper time, dozens of vacationers take showers, one in each compartment. These usually occupy two long rows of shower baths. At that time it is not unusual to listen to singing in various languages and in different tones. If a dozen persons are taking showers, you listen to a dozen moods and ways of singing: lively, sad, joyous, indifferent, lamenting, bellowing, shouting, groaning or grieving.

One, maybe singing in Spanish:

Los cuatro generales,
Los cuatro generales,
Los cuatro generales
Mamita mia
Que se han alzado
Que se han alzado

Para la noche buena
Para la noche buena
Para la noche buena
Mamita mia
Seran ahorcados
Seran ahorcados

Another, perhaps in English:

When Israel was in Egypt land,
Let my people go
Oppressed so hard they could not stand
Let my people go.

Still another, will shift into high opera with:

La donna è mobile
Qual piuma al vento

And a funny thing, nobody jumped from their shower to call him a male chauvinist or words to that effect, for smearing womanhood that way. Perhaps it was because few people knew what he was singing about. (I wonder how the opera companies would sing that part of Rigoletto in the Soviet Union, China, and the other socialist countries).

Once, many, many years ago, I went to a workers' vacation camp for the first time in my life. I was young. As the evening was entering into the night, nature opened up its tremendously big faucet of water in the sky and a voluminous shower came over the grounds and tents of the workers' camp. Someone shouted—"How about going onto the highway in our swimming suits to take a shower?" Nobody answered but in a matter of minutes the highway was covered with young and old—Jews, Italians, Negroes, Mexicans, Spaniards, Cubans, Chinese and Puerto Ricans. We joined arms in twos, fours and sixes and started to sing and sing at the top of our voices to our hearts' content. And nature's shower continued trying to placate our youthful enthusiasm, but it could do nothing about it. It was beyond its control. . . .

> *Avanti popolo*
> *Alla riscossa*
> *Bandiera rossa*
> *Bandiera rossa*

And our voices were more powerful than the intermittent lightning . .

> Long-haired preachers come out every night . . .
> Try to tell you what's wrong and what's right . . .
> And when asked about something to eat
> They will tell you with voices so sweet . .

The shower was converting itself into a torrent. Water kept rolling from our heads and our backs. But we kept singing and laughing and jumping . . . we kept singing under the wonderful shower coming from the sky.

Sometimes when I am home taking a shower I also am given to singing. And I sing those old songs that we sang that night on the highway—black and white and yellow and brown—looking in each other's faces and finding love and optimism in them when the lightning illuminated our heads through the silver curtain of the rain.

When I remember that night on the highway I feel young and happy, and full of hope and optimism again.

39. How To Know the Puerto Ricans

One of the questions that we are most frequently asked is: "How can I get to the Puerto Ricans?" This is not a strang question to ask in a city like greater New York with more than 600,000 Puerto Ricans living, working and struggling along with the rest of our city's inhabitants. This is a question that is crying for a correct answer, not only in our city, but in many other great cities throughout the nation where the Puerto Ricans have gone to live.

We have to admit from the start that we have no complete answer to open the door to the Puerto Ricans' houses, minds and hearts. We have to confess that every day we are adding to that answer by our personal experience, by our going around with our American friends or by listening to what others have done— or have failed to do—in winning entrance to a Puerto Rican home and from there, to their confidence, friendship and love. This, of course, is something that cannot be gotten in one day or in a number of weeks. Sometimes it takes months. Sometimes it takes years.

So, please excuse us if, in presenting what we have learned ourselves or added to our knowledge from the experience of others, we might sound at times a little critical, preachy or even sermonizing. The theme lends itself to committing such errors.

The first thing we must realize is that the Puerto Ricans have been exploited for hundreds of years. That strangers have been knocking at the door of the Puerto Rican nation for centuries always in search of something, to get something or to take away something from Puerto Ricans. This has been done many times with the forceful and openly criminal way of the pirate.

Pirates with such tragically "illustrious" names as Cumberland and Drake. In one of those pirates' assaults around the middle of the 17th century, the bells of the cathedral in San Juan, Puerto

Rico, were stolen and sold by one of their buccaneer ships in a little town known as New Amsterdam just being built along the shores of the Hudson River.

So, in the words of one of my Puerto Rican friends, when one of those 200 percent Americans asks us why do Puerto Ricans have to come to New York? We can answer: "We come to take back our bells."

After the Spanish grandees, the French and English pirates and many other came to deprive us of whatever of value we have in our Puerto Rican land. Many came with the iron fist often hidden in the velvet glove. Many with the unctuous "love" and missionary ways of the do-gooders who come to "help" us. And we always had to listen to the chant that what was being done was "for our own good." Then came the imperialists: the pirates of the "American Century."

So when you come to knock at the door of a Puerto Rican home you will be encountered by this feeling in the Puerto Rican—sometimes unconscious in himself—of having been taken for a ride for centuries. He senses that 99 persons out of a 100 knock at his door because they want something from him and not because they desire to be his friend—a friend solving mutual problems that affect them both.

That is why you must come many times to that door. You must prove yourself a friend, a worker who is also being oppressed by the same forces that keep the Puerto Rican down. Only then will the Puerto Rican open his heart to you. Only then will he ask you to have a cup of black coffee with him in his own kitchen.

Before you come to understand a person, to deserve a people's love, you must know them. You must learn to appreciate their history, their culture, their values, their aspirations for human advancement and freedom.

There is much you can learn by speaking to the Puerto Ricans every time you get a chance at work or in the casual contact of every day life.

We must always be ready to learn from the colonial people. They have much to teach. We do not have to elaborate the point to readers of this column. Their gruelling struggle against economic, political and social oppression has steeled the colonial world and taught its people many a way to combat imperialism and war. We colonial people have also much to learn from the working class of the imperialist countries. But if you want to open that door, don't assume a know-it-all attitude and superior airs just because you were born in the United States. This "superiority" attitude of the imperialist exploiters is unfortunately reflected sometimes in the less developed members of our own working class.

You can acquire much information by reading what is published about the Puerto Ricans in our paper and in the progressive weekly and monthly publications. There are some books with much valuable factual information and many incorrect conclusions. We have to be careful about such books.

40. Soap Box in the Swamps

I like to take a bus on a day off and ride in it until the end of the line. There are many things you can do in a bus besides riding in it. You can see, passing by you, the different aspects of the street or avenue. How the neighborhoods change from affluence to middle class, to poverty and then plain misery at the end of the line.

You can look at the passengers in a bus and try to guess the kind of work they do by the way they dress and the small talk they indulge in with their worker companions. I like to guess how they think by the papers or magazines they are reading or by the way they ask a question of the driver and the gesture they make to accompany the question. Sometimes a little unguarded remark they make to a fellow passenger tells more of their character than what they would care to reveal.

In a bus you can observe and think, think and observe on your day off when you are riding apparently without rhyme or reason, caring little where the bus is actually taking you. At the end of the line you get out. You start walking aimlessly, hard at work with your thoughts as putty for something that you will perhaps write ten years from now. You walk and look and think and you are awakened by the sudden honk of an auto whose driver shouts: "Why t'hell don't you look where you're going?" He would be astonished if he heard the answer that you had in your mind— but that you never uttered. He might call up Kings County if he did hear it. So I smile to the driver and keep on walking, hard at work with my thoughts as material for the dreams that I know will become the reality of tomorrow.

One day I was very lucky. I took a bus that took me to very familiar grounds. When the driver said: "Last stop!" I got off. I walked a few blocks and I came into the grounds of one of the oldest city projects in Brooklyn. I had not been around those

parts for years. The buildings already had that indefinite something that bricks acquire when they have aged a bit. Some
of the walls of the buildings were covered with ivy climbing
almost to the top of their roofs, giving the appearance of a college
building in a small New England town. I sat on one of the
benches and gave myself to the joy of observing a dozen children
playing in one of the project's playgrounds. This brain of
mine, which insists upon not stopping to think for one minute,
did not want me to have a moment for rest and enjoyment, while
watching the children at play.

"What will these children be when they grow up?" My brain
started to ask me.

"Why cannot all poor children in this city have playgrounds
like these and apartments in projects in which to live with their
families?" one part of me insisted on asking. And I got up
from the bench and started to walk again from building to building remembering things that happened right there many, many
years ago.

"Why don't you let the man rest for a while?" another part of
me asked the insisting part. "Don't you see the man is resting?
And you had to come and butt in with your questions and make
him get up from his bench to walk and walk and walk! Let him
alone for awhile, will you?"

So I said "thanks" to that part of me for its consideration and
sat down on another bench near the entrance to one of the apartment buildings.

I saw one of the caretakers of the grounds with his uniform
and his tools of work. He knew immediately that I did not live
in the project. "Beautiful day."—The centuries old phrase to open
up a conversation. "Yes it is." I answered more or less following
the formula. Then I added something new. "A nice project you
have here."

"Oh yes, this is one of the oldest projects in Brooklyn." Then
the caretaker went into statistics telling me about the buildings,
playgrounds, the auditorium, the child care center and the many
other facilities offered to the tenants. The caretaker saw I was
very interested.

"Do you know something about how it came to pass that the city decided to build this project here? The history of its origin?" I inquired.

"No, I don't. All I know is what I see here." After cleaning a bit around the bench where I was sitting he said: "Good day."

"Good day." I answered completing the formula that started with "Beautiful day today."

The caretaker went about his chores. The pigeons came to stare at me and ask me in their cooing language: "Where are the peanuts?" To which I answered the best way I could while they flocked around in their nimble short steps. "Sorry I forgot to bring peanuts. You see I don't come around here very often." And the pigeons seemed to understand, as they left me working with my thoughts of far-off times and actions that took place many years ago.

I started to remember the swamps and the dirty streets and wooden houses of "Hooverville" construction and appearance that were on the site of that very same project forty years ago during prohibition days and when F.D.R. came to the White House for the first time.

In those days the first chapters were written in the creation and development of the very idea of a project on that site. These were the chapters that the caretakers did not know.

I even remember the smell of the stagnating waters in those swamps that were where the project now is. Many an evening we went to the "homes" in the middle of those swampy lands with a few hundred leaflets very poorly run off on an old battered mimeograph machine. The leaflet called for a meeting at a central point of all those swampy dirk dirty streets. It announced that there would be speakers from the Communist Party, the Unemployment Councils and "other well known speakers" from the community. They will demand that a project be built right there in those swamps. That's what the leaflet said.

How well I remember the folding speaker's stand and the long pole with the American flag that we tied to the stand with two pieces of heavy brown string. Sometimes we did not have a stand. We just came with a box given to us by some grocer. From that box we spoke and our voices pierced the night as if we were speaking to fifteen thousand people in Madison Square Garden. But as we looked around the box from where we stood addressing the "public" we counted them. They were always the same customary half dozen faithfuls who night after night accompanied us wherever we called a meeting.

But in this swampy district of Brooklyn we did not really worry much about having just half a dozen people around the stand. We knew that they were sitting somewhere inside their wooden houses, their makeshift "Hooverville homes" listening to what the "communists" had to say outside.

One speaker succeeded the other. One spoke about the need for public housing. The other spoke about the need for welfare help. And as one speaker succeeded the other there was a very attentive silence coming from the void of the night. A silence that spoke to you in a very significant way. A silence more eloquent than words. Only once in a long while you listened to a voice coming through the dark . . .

"Commuuunissstaaaa!"

"Cooommuuunissttl"

And as the speaker kept on talking in English, Spanish or Italian, you listened intently to see if the significant silence was going to be broken by some one joining the sole voice of redbaiting. Nobody else repeated the word. They just kept silent. Listening, listening to what the "communists" had to say outside.

As we kept coming the same day every week, to the same corner, many started to leave their "homes" and came to join our half dozen faithfuls near the speaker's stand. After that we circulated petitions house to house. More and more people signed hundreds of petitions. Delegations went to the mayor. Many meetings were organized in big halls. The people were on the move for welfare benefits and public housing until both these things, that today are taken very much for granted, were won for the people, organized by a handful of men and women who all over the country dared to believe in the people's strength.

Far be it from me to assert that these victories were won only because of the efforts of the Communists in those days. But we cannot deny either that their activities counted a great deal in the winning of these victories.

As I kept sitting on the bench looking at the project already old as projects go these days, I kept remembering about those evenings of leaflet distribution and street corner meetings in these very grounds where I was sitting many, many years ago. And many names kept coming to my mind who, in their big or small ways, helped to convert many dreams into realities. Hours must have passed in this kind of reverie that I was having with memories of actions a little older than the project I was contemplating.

Suddenly I was brought back to the present. "Hello, Mr. Colon! Long time no see!" The man addressing me was undoubtedly Puerto Rican. A Puerto Rican who had surely been living in New York since childhood. He had almost no accent in his pronunciation.

"Hello," I said, without remembering who the man was. He seemed to have noticed it. "Don't you remember me?"

"To tell you the truth, I don't remember."

"Well, it has been so many years. I lived in the old wooden house that used to be over in that corner of that street. You knew my mother well. She believed in everything you said when you used to speak around here many years ago.

"I have lived in the project for the last twenty-five years. Married. My name is——."

Then I remembered him. He was one of the few who did not believe in our campaign for a project in the swamps.

in Memory of Ana Mercado
Her Husband, Father, Four
Children, and Other Victims
of Arson for Profit.
A.M.O.R.

41. My Private Hall of Fame

When I hear of a person who has done something, no matter how small or great, to advance the cause of human liberation and understanding, I say to myself that he or she is entitled to be included in my private Hall of Fame.

Yes, I have a private Hall of Fame. I have photographs of men and women—they don't have to be world famous or even nationally so. If I have seen for myself or heard from reliable sources that they had done a noble deed no matter how small, I start hunting for a suitable photograph of that person for my private Hall of Fame. So, you see, nobody can accuse me of the cult of personality. But they can accuse me of the cult of many personalities.

There are great men and women in all walks of life, from the humblest to the most sublime exploits of sacrifice for human rights and happiness. Sometimes they pass through life almost unnoticed. When we say that man is good and great, what we are really saying is that in every man and in every woman there is a spark of that collective goodness and greatness that humanity worked on and developed throughout the ages.

So I am always on the alert for that little spark—no matter how little—or how great—in men and women all around me. It is one of life's greatest thrills to be present when one of these little bits of human decency or courage or what have you actually occurs right in front of your very eyes. When it does and I am around, I always try to get a photograph of the persons to better remember the deed.

Sometimes I fail. And I cannot get a suitable picture until months, sometimes years later.

I have been searching for quite some time for a photograph of Jesus Maria Sanroma, the well known Puerto Rican concert pianist. Sanroma was brought up in the town of Fajardo, Puerto Rico. I was told by a friend born in that town that on one of the visits that the great pianist made there, he did not hire a hall for the town's elite to go and sit comfortably and listen to him play. Instead, he placed a concert piano in the open spacious church courtyard and invited the whole town to come and listen. For many hours, he played, graciously giving all the encores asked by the people.

A few years ago at a national gathering of U.S. teachers at Madison Square Garden, Jesus Maria Sanroma was one of the invited artists. The master of ceremonies referred to the growth and development of the union of teachers in the United States. Then he continued, presenting Sanroma to the public. As he was about to sit at the piano to interpret Gershwin as only he can do, Sanroma shouted into the crowded Garden: "I am a union member too." And putting his hand into his coat pocket he took his union card and hoisted it over his head as a flag worthy of waving over him. A man who can do little things like that deserves to be included in my private Hall of Fame.

The standard of inclusion in this private Hall of Fame that I have consists not only of great deeds, but little deeds that augur far more famed doings to come in the future.

Another photograph that I have been seeking for many years is one of Diosa Costello, the Puerto Rican dancer and singer who played the part of Bloody Mary, after Juanita Hall left "South Pacific." I don't want Diosa's picture because she played Bloody Mary in South Pacific. I will tell you why I want it.

One evening at an elaborate dancing contest in Madison Square Garden—a contest called "Harvest Moon" by the Publicity Department of a New York paper—Diosa was introduced as one of the professional attractions, to sing and dance before the contest itself started. A sort of stimulation for those coming up the dance ladder.

The Garden was full to the rafters. The bombastic master of ceremonies, in the usual hollow voice that they assume on such occasions and with an all-encircling wave of his hands and arms announced: "And now, I am going to present to youuuu . . . thaat teerrifiiic Cuban bombshell, Diooosssaaa Costello . . . accompanied by the great Cuban OOOrchestraa of Juanito Sanabria."

As if moved by an electric clock, Diosa waved both her arms in a sign for silence while all the big flashlights of the Garden were playing on her beautiful figure. In a deep clear, clamorous voice, she cried: "I am a Puerto Rican, and proud of it. Juanito Sanabria and his orchestra are also Puerto Ricans." Long, sonorous applause followed her words.

She was not saying that she did not want to be Cuban—a glorious and proud people. Diosa was just saying that she was Puerto Rican and proud of it. That, in a New York atmosphere of an artificial anti-Puerto Rican hysteria, inflated by the "confidential" calumnies of yellow journalists, was something to be appreciated and admired.

Diosa was not only proud that she was a Puerto Rican but also proud of being a product of that much maligned and misrepresented "El Barrio"—Puerto Rican Harlem.

For years I have been looking for a good photograph of Paul Robeson. Some nights or early mornings I come in very tired. I love to look at the understanding faces in the photographs of the men and women, living and dead, looking at me from the walls of the winding staircase. As I say to myself that I must cut out so many late meetings—I am not so young anymore—I struggle up the stairs held to the glimmering light of a far off vision of a united and happy humanity in socialism. I would like to have Paul Robeson's photograph, together with the rest of the pictures, one of those nights or early mornings when I come home very tired. Never can tell. Perhaps I might be able to induce him, at that hour, to give me a private concert. Just for me and all the other men and women on the walls of my home.

I will ask him to start with the Peat-bog Soldiers, in that language which I don't understand and yet the meaning of the song is so clear to me. Maybe while I brood on one of the steps of that old winding rickety staircase of mine and take off my shoes so that I would make less noise as I renew my climb, I will ask him to sing some more. I will ask for another song in the strong, sonorous language of Cervantes and the Spanish Guerrillas. A song from the Spanish Civil War. I will ask him to sing "Los Cuatro Generales," with that prophetic last line: "Seran ahorcados. Seran ahorcados." ("They shall be hanged. They shall be hanged.") And I will notice and relish that over emphasis and definite assurance that Paul always gives to his Spanish as he sings that line in that song.

And as I squeeze myself nicely, easily and quietly under the cold blanket so that I will not wake up my wife, that last line of the song will be following me from Paul's *picture*. And I, tired but happy will go into a slumber. And then into a sure and confident sleep.

42. Books That Never Get Returned

There is nothing so difficult as returning a book. My wife's maxim is, "A book loaned is a book lost." I would not go as far as that. I would say though that if I could have been present when Francis Bacon wrote: "Some books are to be tasted, others to be swallowed and some few to be chewed and digested," I would have suggested that he add: "and some books are to be read and returned."

On this question of returning books we have borrowed, we should not make any exceptions. It has happened to me. It happens to you. It happens to all of us—lenders and borrowers of books. You "borrow a book for a few days" from "a very good friend." Before you know it the few days are converted into weeks, the weeks into months, the months. . . . And still the book borrowed "for a few days" remains—many a time unread—acclimatized to the methodical confusion of the new environment.

I borrow a book and carelessly turn the leaves as I ride the subway home. I open the door and place the book on the first chair I can find. All the characters inside the book sit there on that chair waiting for me to pick them up and introduce them to my mind. After the second cup of coffee, I bring the book with me into that stately second hand chair I bought in an auction sale.

How well I remember that auction sale! I was enticed to enter by the siren call of the auctioneer reaching to the sidewalk where I thought I was free from the influence of any hidden persuading. How well I remember that day! The voice came, velvety and breezy over the microphone right onto the sidewalk: "Here you have, ladies and gentlemen, a unique example of 19th century furniture. A chair in which to do your reading in splendor. A chair with delicately carved legs and green soft cushioned arms, seat and back. A comfortable reading chair for today made by the exquisite artisans of centuries gone by. . . ."

159

While he was talking I kept saying to myself: NO, No, No, No. And yet I kept unconsciously moving nearer and nearer to the auctioneers' counter.

There, as I prepared myself to start reading the latest borrowed book, was this chair—I should say this monstrosity—in all its ancient magnificence of fringes, curlicues and brass knobs. Sometimes, as I am about to sit in it, I grow very angry with myself just thinking how this auctioneer blinded me into buying it. There it is now, hogging the largest part of my room, right by that other futuristic distortion of an ultra modern lamp that somebody favored me with on my last birthday. When I sit down on that chair and under this multishaped lamp to read, I feel like a man dangling between two centuries with a book in his hands.

Sitting in a synthesis of what is really an example of pompous Victorian bad taste, prepared to read this borrowed book which I expect to return someday, I think of the folly of lending books, especially those that are out of print or because of some other reason are hard to buy, borrow or spirit from somebody else's shelf. I am using the word "spirit" to avoid another more direct and truthful term.

Yes, there are friends—very good friends—who would not hesitate to spirit a book from under your nose in your own home if they think they really need it and they cannot get it anywhere else. They are good humored and nice about it too. Their rationalization goes something like this: "He has the book that I need for finishing the work I am involved with now. He is not using the book. He has so many books that it will take perhaps a year or more before he notices it. By that time I shall have finished with it, bring it and place it right where I took it from and nobody will know the difference."

But of course, they never return the book.

They mean to return it at some future day. But one time out of a hundred they do. They seldom return it, because a book is one of the most difficult things to return.

So, when some of my book-ravaging friends come to visit me, I always take them to the door and in a good natured way I say to them when they have their hats and coats on: "My, my, but you are certainly growing fat these days!" And with these words I embrace them as closely as I can. They give me a knowing smile as if to say: "I fooled you tonight didn't I?" I return the knowing smile. I know that the next time I go to visit them they will come to the door and embrace me likewise.

Books grow on you. They become part of you. Borrowed books intermingle with your own until they form a familiar pattern on the walls of your room.

Sometimes I need a book. I know that at a certain period of my life, I had that book on my shelves. I do not remember who borrowed the book the last time.

So, in the middle of a group of my booklover friends I say absent-mindedly-like, "Gee, I need to have a copy of book WXZ. I need it for just a few days." More often than you can imagine, somebody comes to the front and tells you: "I have that book. I'll lend you my copy." And more often than not, the copy that is "lent" turns out to be your own copy of the book that was "borrowed" from you so long ago that both you and the borrower had forgotten all about it.

Books are indeed the most difficult thing to return.

43. Reading in the Bathtub

In one of our sketches, we contrasted the pleasures of reading in bed with those of reading in the bathtub. We pointed out that the pleasures of reading in the bathtub should not be disposed of lightly. Some of our friends seemed to have doubled the existence of the bathtub readers. And I affirm that there is such a breed in this world. I am one of them.

Most every household has a bathtub reader. Of course many of them don't really do their reading in the bathtub. But, as I said before, almost every household has one such specimen. They are the desperation and delight of all concerned. They usually take hold of the bath room during those "five minute" periods that often stretch to a full hour from seven to eight every morning. Meanwhile a line of half-robed towel-necked, long-suffering souls patiently wait outside the bath room door waiting for him to finish the last bundle of comic books he bought the night before.

But don't misunderstand me. All bath room readers are not of the comic book variety. You have those who go in and lock themselves in that most important room in the house from seven to eight in the morning, with Gibbon's *Decline and Fall of the Roman Empire,* just as if they were going to scan the latest invitation for the next Saturday night party. And when they go in with something like Gibbon's "Decline and Fall," only a collective, BANG! BANG! BANG! threatening the fall of the bath room door will yank them from their leisurely reading.

But these are not the kind of bathtub readers I am going to write about. The ones I have been describing in the previous paragraphs are the inconsiderate ones. No self respecting bathtub reader will read in the tub between the hours of seven and eight in the morning. Although, of course, there are some who think that indulging in a half hour reading between seven and eight is nothing to perturb anybody. There are differences of opinion on this point.

162

But let us go into the science and art of bath-tub reading itself. First I have to fill the bathtub with very warm water until the level of the water reaches that grated circle right under the water faucet—the grated circle only plumbers know why it was placed there. Then I lie down in the bottom of the bathtub, with my hands holding the book outside the water. As I keep on reading, the water gets cold.

Then I pull the plug and let some of the already cold water run down the drain, as I watch the water line go down on the walls of the bathtub. You cannot read during this brief period of drain-ing some water, plugging back the drain and letting the warm water run until it fills the tub again to the desired level. If you keep on reading while the water is running out, you may find your-self in a bathtub without a drop of warm liquid around you. Then you start getting chills. The hair on your arms and legs starts getting up from your moist skin and a cold feverish feeling starts taking possession of all your body. Most uncomfortable, I should say. That is why you should stop reading for a minute until you properly refill the bath tub with extra warm water. The most you could do during this minute is to hold the book or magazine you are reading in your dry left hand while you dilly-dally with the plug and the drain with your wet right hand.

As I am about to go back to a sitting position, I dry my right hand with one of the two beautifully embroidered towels that a good friend gave us on our thirtieth wedding anniversary. They were hung by my wife on two aluminum rod fixtures on the wall. These are the two towels nobody dares to touch. They are the sacred cows of our home. (Why is it that we must have sacred cows even in our homes?). These two towels are the grandparents in respectability and untouchability of that pair of towels marked HIS and HERS that are usually given to newlyweds. Their only utility is to entice you in an "I-dare-you" sort of a way when you come in to take a quick shave in the morning and have forgotten to bring your laundromat-looking rag of a towel into the bath room with you. Aside from that, these HIS and HERS towels don't have any useful purpose but to extract a hypocritical and tepid "How nice!" from one of the intimate "friends" of the bride or groom on a curious inspection tour of the three-room apartment very early in the morning after the newlyweds' wedding night.

But on an occasion like this—when you are reading in the bath tub—you find a psychological use for these immaculate towels. You just pass your wet right hand, lightly but firmly, over one until you have the sensation that you have really dried your hand. Nobody but the most cleanliness-conscious eagle eye will ever be the wiser that one of the two sacred cows were lightly patted with a wet hand. When you do this, you will find that your whole body is filled with a sense of freedom and exhilaration. You will feel like hollering to the world: "Down with sacred cows!"

Now you are ready to resume your reading again. From the sitting position, you go back nicely and easily, to your lying position at the bottom of the bathtub. You lie in the newly refilled tub with your two hands and part of the forearms outside the water. The book or magazine securely held by both your hands.

Before we go any further, we must say that reading material for the bathtub must be chosen not only for content but for the physical form of the book or magazine. They have to be wide enough so that when you find such a profound sentence as "A rose is a rose is a rose," you could place the book on the edge of the bath tub face down while you go into deep thinking unhampered by any other preoccupation but your thoughts. Here I concede that you could perhaps indulge in scratching one foot with the other slowly and absentmindedly under the warm water while still engaged in deep thinking.

Just as there are all other kinds of organizations—Divorcees Anonymous, The Society for the Preservation of Decorated Egg Shells, etc.—there should be a national organization with yearly conventions and for all those who enjoy reading in the bathtub. I am sure that many unknown factors and unsung pleasures would come to be better known when delegates from say, Alaska and Florida, present reports on their reading-in-the-bath-tub experiences.

Just as you have publishing houses that have specialized in books for this and that and the other, just as you have a dozen companies that publish millions of books that fit very neatly into the reader's pocket, it would not be considered far-fetched if some book company would issue editions for those who like to read in the bath tub. I suggest that a special bath tub edition of Omar Khayam reads:

> *A jug of wine*
> *A loaf of bread*
> *And thou*
> *Besides me singing in the bathtub.*
> *Oh, bathtub were paradise enow.*

instead of the better known translations of this stanza in vogue for the last one hundred years.

There are all kinds of readers besides the ones just mentioned. There are the "over the shoulder readers"—a rather despised flock. Then you have the subway readers, those who stick their heads between your face and what you are reading right from their adjacent seats. There is the well known heavy traffic reader, who reads Nietzsche's *Thus Spake Zarathustra* while zig-zagging through traffic on Broadway and 42nd Street.

And there are the "readers" who don't read and who swear on a stack of Marx's *Capital* that they have read and studied a specific book or pamphlet, when they haven't even glanced at it. You can excuse even the absent-minded reader who insists on keeping on reading while crossing Times Square. But the "reader" who does not read and says he does, that one you cannot excuse.

44. What Shall I Write About?

Here I am, blankly looking at a piece of paper, pencil in hand, back from my vacation, thinking about what I should write about this week. I am still with that after-vacation feeling. You know. The one that calls for a vacation right after the one you've just had.

I can still see the drops of morning dew resting on the velvety green leaves, like great big diamonds on a surface of emeralds as I stepped out to take a long deep breath of non-slum air.

I could yet remember the charming young girl, so very conscious of her emerging womanhood, dressed in the very latest swim-suit creation from Gimbel's basement, going down to the lake to "mermaid" it with the less esthetic pikes, perches and flounders.

I can still see the serious looking young man with heavy rimmed glasses and a book under his arm—a book that he never seemed to have time to open up and read.

I can still hear the young boys and girls gathered around me at the Children's hour, actually laughing their heads off at my simple card tricks and my jokes of 1920 vintage.

But you must realize, my dear readers, that with my mind on the green open valleys and the mountains and the lakes, unable to get hold of a *Daily Worker* and hardly any New York papers and without the day-to-day contact of the millions of people of this bustling, crowded, whirling New York, my mind has to be more or less blank at least for this first week.

Speaking about papers, there are none like our New York papers. I mean the best of our New York papers with our *Daily Worker* heading them all.

One day we went to the town nearest to the place where my wife and I were staying. Just for curiosity I bought a copy of the town's paper. Most everything in it was town news of who was born, who got married and who died. What attracted my attention immediately was a four column cut on the first page of this little paper. It represented the mayor with a great big pair of scissors in his hands cutting a ribbon that was to inaugurate traffic over the main passageway of a small new bridge. The mayor was surrounded by other town authorities, all chest forward, with a pompous pose just as the town photographer told him to stand and look. And he looked as if he had built that bridge, alone and unassisted, with his two bare hands.

Which set me to thinking about the thousands of bridges, highways and buildings at which other hot air artists like this small town mayor have cut many other ribbons, giving the impression that they themselves were the ones who built it all. About the draftsmen, mechanics, carpenters, engineers, masons and plain laborers who did the ditch digging and the actual building, not a word.

I always get a restrained laugh, when I see one of these official guys, trowel in hand, in the act of "laying the first stone" for a project or any other building, so cautious that their well-ironed striped pants will not get dirty with a bit of cement. How I would love to see the day when the best concrete worker, carpenter or plumber among those who actually worked on the job, is given the honor of cutting the ribbon on the door of a newly built factory, school, hospital, bridge or highway, presenting in the ceremony at least half a dozen workers like himself who did outstanding work in constructing the building! And that day shall come!

But here am I, still thinking about what I should write in my column today!

Oh, I know that we have plenty of important things to write about. The cult, the transition, the new approach, the errors of right and of left. All these things are important. But you just cannot plunge into them just like that right after you've come back from a vacation.

To tell the truth, I would like to see our people all over America writing more about the mayors of the big and small towns, about the politicians that surround them, about the plain ordinary, non-class conscious butchers, bakers and candlestick makers, and make an effort to discover what makes them tick.

I have a sneaking suspicion that they've got the answers to many of the problems that we are trying to solve.

45. What D'Ya Read?

The other day I was waiting for the train on the subway platform on 59th Street and Eighth Avenue. Force of habit drew me to the newspaper and magazine stand. The rectangular parallel counters with the two rounded ends linking them together, looked to me like a multicolored little ferry boat plodding its course through a sea of people.

I started to read what some of the nationally known monthlies and weeklies were offering this month to their millions of readers. Here are some of the names of the articles, taken at random, from the printed covers of some of these magazines:

"All Women Are Cheats."
"Secrets of Sex Appeal."
"After My Auto Crash."
"He Loved His Family More Than Me."
"Live in Luxury at $45 a Week."
"U. S.—Nation of Weaklings."
"Florida Fantastic Glamour Boom."

I noticed some of the titles of the paper-covered books offered to the public at these newsstands. Here are the names of some of these books:

"Apache Ambush."
"Gun of the Lawless."
"The Man Who Could Not Shudder."

When I read the names of books such as the ones printed above, I recalled the saying in one of Bacon's short essays: "Some books are to be tasted, others to be swallowed, and some few to be chewed and digested." Had he lived to see the trash offered to the public in dozens of magazines and hundreds of books today, I am sure that he would have added: "And some books and magazines are to be speedily thrown into the waste basket."

I thought that I was seeing all this for the first time. But, as if awakened suddenly from a bad dream, I started to change from surprise to amazement when I realized that this sort of reading material is being offered to the general public from week to week and from year to year all through these great United States.

I want you to know that I did not pick the names of these articles from the "down the gutter confidential" type of magazines. These written pieces are included in some of the so-called best slick monthlies and weeklies.

At the sight of this tremendous wave of escapist and subtly disguised pornographic literature on the stands, let us pledge to continue buying the progressive magazines and papers, which have a small circulation and are always on the verge of disappearing for lack of funds. For these progressive publications have something that the big ones with their millions in circulation and millions of dollars in advertisements will never have. And that is a sense of the grandeur and beauty and the freedom of man and his future.

Let us continue to buy the books that, with grim determination and sacrifice, are being written and printed by the independent and other well known far-seeing publishers. They are certainly helping to mould the bright future that is to come.

46. The Visitor

We met on 14th Street. After so many years without seeing her, I had forgotten her name. All that I was sure of was that she had a baby daughter whom she brought to meetings years ago when she was very active in one of the fraternal organizations in Harlem.

I wanted to say "hello-goodbye," as I was late for a class at school. But she insisted on talking about the good old days when we had Puerto Rican progressive organizations in Harlem with ladies' auxiliaries—or Women's Committees—of 40 and 50 members. How things had changed! I assured her with all the conviction that I could muster that those days would come again . . . bigger and better.

To change the subject I asked, "and how is the little baby daughter?" "Oh, you should see her now! She is a nice looking young lady; and can she dance! I mean DANCE." And she emphasized this last word before she flung herself into a more detailed description of her daughter's dancing abilities.

"I wish you could come to our place and see her dance, one of these evenings. Perhaps a few evenings. In order to really appreciate her, you must see her dance more than once." Then she added, "Will you come next Friday? I really want you to tell me whether she has talent.' ' After elevating me to the category of judge of dancing, there was only one answer to her invitation: "Yes!"

They lived in one of the worst slum areas in the East Bronx. The building was at least 100 years old . . . One of those buildings that are an affront to the beautiful art of architecture. The wooden stairs were lopsided and dirty. As your feet pressed down on the steps, all kinds of rickety-rackety sounds came from inside the boards which seemed to be strenuously opposed to being awakened from the sleep of centuries.

170

As you entered the apartment you came into a short dark hall that connected the entrance with the kitchen. At the left there was the bathroom and at the right, a bedroom. The farthest end of the kitchen led you into the parlor.

The baby daughter who used to whimper and cry at 9 P.M. on the dot when her mother took her to meetings, had grown into a young lady of harmonious beauty. She was brown skinned, statuesque, graceful in her movements and lithe in her step. She had a wistful smile that enveloped her face, revealing a warm healthy personality. She unconsciously danced as she walked around the parlor. We talked for a while.

Finally I reminded myself that I came not to talk but to see her dance. I asked her if she would dance for me. As she started to walk towards the victrola her mother said: "You'd better close the door between the kitchen and the parlor, so that 'She' cannot come in."

Perhaps the mother wanted me not to be disturbed by the presence of anybody else . . . a neighbor, a friend, another member of the family, I thought to myself. And I relaxed in a deep old chair ready to enjoy or suffer for the next 15 minutes, the dancing of the young lady.

After carefully closing the door between the kitchen and the parlor, the daughter placed a long-playing record of sections of ballet music on the victrola.

She danced to one of them. As she kept herself in the position of the last note, she seemed to ask with her half-opened eyes and with the two dimples in her cheeks: "How do you like it?" Instead of answering her I asked in return: "And where did you learn all that?" She answered with just one word: "Television."

Other evenings followed during which the daughter exhibited her skill in the many variations of the Spanish and Latin American dances. This young dancer really had talent. I told the mother so. She took it as if my judgment came from the mouth of Jose Limon, or John Martin.

One evening the girl was interpreting the Waltz of the Flowers as I was sitting in the soft old chair that by now had been unofficially assigned to me whenever I came.

The mother was reclining on the sofa enjoying the sylph-like movements of her daughter as she softly and gracefully let her body flow through the air.

On this particular evening the door between the kitchen and the parlor had been left ajar. Little by little, emerging from the silence of the darkened kitchen, the outline of an animal the size of a small cat began to be distinguishable.

First I could only notice the snout with which the animal was trying to push himself through the door opening. Then "her" body started to come forward.

I noticed then that it was not a cat at all, but a tremendously big rat with long grimy black-brown hair and two bead-like eyes peering at you from under two bushy eyebrows.

Its steps were sure as if walking on familiar ground. Mother and daughter must have noticed the revulsion on my face.

Suddenly they saw that the kitchen door was open. They looked around and saw the rat leisurely promenading through the legs of the sofa and the chairs in the parlor.

I instinctively took off one of my loafer shoes and aiming it at the rat's head let go with all the power in my arm. But I am not a Reuben Gomez nor a Don Newcombe!* The rat looked at me disdainfully for a few seconds and then continued on its way as unconcerned as before.

It was the mother who got the rat out of the parlor. By the way she reacted it seemed that she had done it before. She took a heavy stick that stood unnoticed in one of the corners and sometimes hitting, sometimes pushing the rat, she finally forced it out of the parlor into the kitchen where we all followed her until the rat disappeared through a great big hole in the wall near the kitchen sink.

"I have been telling the landlord to fix that hole for the last three months. I have been holding the rent until he fixes it. Come."

And with this, she led me back into the parlor closing the door securely after us.

---

* Famous baseball pitchers. Gomez is a Puerto Rican.

47. Red Roses for Me

The two roses were there on top of my old battered desk when I came in. Their delicate rings of petals invited your touching them. Their long green stems, embroidered with diminutive leaves, kept themselves erect as if they knew that at their ends was pending a very precious thing: a rose.

Two red roses for me. They were surrounded by papers in many languages coming from far off lands. Papers that told the thousand times told tale of man's red blood being poured out in the struggle to end the exploitation of man by man.

Red roses for me. I wonder who placed them there. Just two red roses on top of my battered desk.

I went over to get the glass jar out of which I ate the fruit salad that I bought for my lunch yesterday. I washed the jar nicely, put some fresh water in it and then I immersed the stems of the two roses in the jar half filled with fresh water. Keats' Grecian urn could not look any more beautiful than my two red roses perfuming all, from the fruit salad glass jar on top of my old battered desk.

The mail comes in and I read one postal card. The whole message is roughly hand printed in capital letters with this literary "gem":

"YOU DAM COMMIES, WHY DON'T YOU
CLOSE YOUR DAM PAPER AND GO
BACK TO ROOSIA."

I just smile and become very happy. Because that postal card showed me that the fascist-minded and plain reactionary elements in our midst are being hurt and are concerned about our paper's message to the people.

I carefully observe the color of the two roses in the fruit salad jar. What a beautiful color red is! Red.

Let me read you one more note received in our morning mail. It says:

Brothers:

I will always be with you. I admire your courageous effort in publishing such necessary papers as the *Daily* and the *Sunday Worker* are today. But unfortunately, because of circumstances that I cannot mention, I have to ask you to cancel my subscription immediately.

Fraternally,

. . . .

My smile was not joyous any more after I finished reading this short note, I got up, I took the fruit salad jar with my two hands and inhaled the deep fragrant perfume of the roses. Then, in order to admire their redness the better from afar, I returned the jar and roses to where they were before at the far right corner of my old battered desk.

Let me read you still another letter of the many we receive. This reads:

Gentlemen:

After reading your last editorial on——— I came to the conclusion that you are barking up the wrong tree and that your paper has left forever the camp of socialism.

Please cancel my subscription.

Respectfully,

. . . .

When a good progressive person writing to us starts her or his letter addressing us as "Gentlemen" and closing with "Respectfully" instead of "Fraternally" or "Comradely," I know that person is very sore.

Letters like the one above are written when the one writing it is feeling very hot under the collar or dead set on how a question should have been formulated and presented in the paper according to him. When she or he reads that our paper's position is not exactly the one that, in their opinion, should prevail, a letter to cancel the subscription is sent to the paper.

There are sometimes, of course, other motives. Fortunately we receive only a small handful of such letters. We are happy to report that, even of this handful of very good readers, most of them write back to renew after they have had time to cool off and consider all the angles.

And when we receive a renewal from one who had left us for any of a number of reasons, I feel as if one more red rose, fragrant and beautiful, has been placed by somebody on top of my old battered desk.

Then there is the reader whom you find in the street, at a social or at a lecture or play.

"Hello!"

"Hello!"

"How are things at the paper?"

"So, so. You know how things are these days. We . . ."

"Yes, yes, I know. By the way, that column that you wrote a few weeks ago . . . I meant to write to you telling you how good (or how lousy) it was, but I never got around to doing it. Anyhow, know it now. It was very good (or very lousy). *Hasta la vista*." Which, of course is better than not writing at all.

But still, I would like more readers to write. To send us brickbats or red roses. The bricks would be good to remind us that we have a long way to go on that road to a perfection which is never achieved. Bricks have the salutary effect of arousing us from a sort of self-complacency with ourselves. Besides, bricks are very good to be used as book-ends. Bricks have a simple, rugged nature. And they are red. Red roses, besides being simple and red, have a lovely form and delicacy and perfume. And they look nice in a fruit-salad jar.

48. It Happened One Winter's Night

I still remember that snowy night during the Christmas holidays many more years ago than I care to remember.

There was a friend way out in Long Island whose Christmas celebrations—Puerto Rican style—were justly famous.

I asked a mutual friend—an automobile mechanic—who had a car, if he would like to drive to this friend's house.

It was a really dark, cold snowy night. Nevertheless he agreed to drive. It was rough going. I did not know how to drive. He had to go very carefully and slowly as you could hardly see half a dozen feet beyond the front of the car

New snow was coming down upon the petrified snow already in the streets for days, making white multiformed whirlwinds that eventually came to rest upon the glistening snow covered pavements.

As we came to the Grand Central Parkway where there was hardly an auto to be seen on such a night, my friend who was doing all the driving, started to talk.

"It would be a very nice thing to be like you, Jesus. To be able to get up and talk, just like that"—and he accompanied his words with a quick snap of his fingers. "Talk about Greece and Rome . . . and Russia. Or about music, or poetry or . . ." and he seemed to be looking for more representative words to express the various fields of knowledge in which he thought I was at home.

Flattery is an alluring and poisonous thing. I knew I did not deserve one-fifth of all the honeyed words that I was hearing. Yet I did not stop him. I did not stop him because, no matter how safe you think you are from this kind of sickness, there always remains something of the old upbringing, of the previous ways of looking at life and at yourself. That is, if you are human.

It is a sickness one must never stop fighting.

I also did not stop him because I recognized in the words of

176

my mechanic friend the unspoiled and innocent respect for another worker like himself who he thought had acquired in his spare moments a certain amount of erudition.

It seemed to me that it happened to be his real and honest opinion, unfortunately not based on real and concrete facts.

I felt like telling him that all the learning, so-called, that I had was acquired listening to the tobacco workers from outside one of the tobacco factory windows when I was a boy in my hometown in Puerto Rico.

That this was followed by an unorganized, if abundant, reading at public libraries and by a few hundred pamphlets and outlines published by Haldeman-Julius and such others, plus a few books, pamphlets, and periodicals of serious reading in the social sciences.

I wanted to tell him what a hodge-podge, what a Spanish omelet of half baked ideas about everything I still had surrounding what I hoped was clear Marxist thinking. But I remained quiet.

My automobile mechanic friend continued driving and speaking in the same vein for a few more minutes.

We left Grand Central Parkway and started south until we reached Hempstead Turnpike. Suddenly the car started to shake backward and forward, first with a lot of noise then less noisily until it came to a full stop.

"What happened?" I asked my friend

"Something must have gone wrong out there," he answered pointing to the motor in front of the car. Then he added: "I must get out and see what it's all about."

He took a flashlight from the small compartment on the right underneath the windshield and after looking for the tools he thought were to be needed from the car trunk, he came to the front and started to look inside the motor part.

While I was holding the flashlight as he was fixing what was wrong, I remained deeply in thought.

I knew it was useless for me to try to be of any real help to my mechanic friend. I did not know the first thing about cars. I imagined myself driving an automobile in a night such as that when, all of a sudden, the car should stop on me. Dead in the middle of nowhere. What would I do? Where would I start? I, who did not know the difference between a crankshaft and a spark plug. Shivers went over my body just to think of it.

After a few seconds of shaking off the snow that had accumulated on his clothes, my friend bounded into his seat back of the steering wheel and closed the door after him. I came through the other front door seating myself beside him.

"Everything is OK now. Real nasty out there, wasn't it?" my friend said.

The car started easily and smoothly, then a little faster until we were again happily on our way. After a little silence my friend was getting ready to start speaking again.

"As I was saying . . ."

This time I cut him short, by introducing a new theme in the ensuing conversation.

49. "I Made It"—"I Sold It"—"I Bought It"

Have you seen that advertisement in the subway or the bus? There are three squares. In each square there is a drawing representing the figure of a person. The first figure represents a well groomed fiftyish looking man, a picture of health and satisfaction, of rest and prosperity. In his well manicured fingers he is holding an article: a brand. Underneath this never-have-worked figure of a man there is a sign reading. "I made it!" referring to the product—the brand—he is holding in his hands.

In the middle square there is the figure of a slick young man, obviously a salesman. He has the same product in his hands. Under his figure there is another sign. It reads: "I sold it!" At the extreme right, there is the figure of a young housewife with the identical product in her hands. At the bottom of this figure there is a line reading: "I bought it!"

Now ask yourself the next time you enter a subway or a bus and gaze at that advertisement: "What is wrong with this picture?" You will, of course, discover the glaring fact that the well groomed, well dressed and manicured . . . gentleman in the first square has not made anything in his whole life. He looks like a man who does nothing but clip coupons while changing from villas to sumptuous hotels as the mood strikes him and the seasons change.

The first time I saw the advertisement and read the "Made it!" underneath the suave arrogant picture of a "man" I could not restrain myself. I just stood in front of the sign, and pointing my finger directly at the picture, said loud enough for everybody to hear: "He Made It! Ha, ha, ha." Some people looked at me as if I were crazy. A man talking to a sign in an advertisement! "What is this country coming to!" "People are nuts these days!" I heard an old lady muttering to herself.

I would like to see the reaction of a steelworker or any worker from the basic industries really noticing that ad in a bus going say, from Chicago to Gary, Indiana. I bet that when he reads: "I Made It!" coming from the mouth of the well dressed esquire, the worker would exclaim: "Sez who!" or words to that effect, perhaps more direct and stronger. "He Made It!" The nerve of the guy! As if you could really make anything in striped pants and an elaborate vest and tails! Impossible to do any work, to make anything in such an outfit! You just try it sometime. Such attire is good for exploitation but not for work. Don't you think?

"I Made It" Ha, ha, ha.

"If you ask me"-a young garment worker straphanging besides me said—"all the old fox does is wait until you and thousands like you finish your day's work, to rob you of half or more of whatever you made during your eight-hour day's work."

And you can imagine the size of his loot just by multiplying the money he actually steals from you every day by the number of workers in your factory.

If this highway robbery of every one of the workers in your factory is going on every day among all the other workers in every factory and place where work is done, you can imagine the millions that the factory owners, bankers and financiers like the gentleman in the picture squeeze from the sweat and blood of the workers every day. And still he has the nerve to be pictured in a subway advertisement claiming: "I Made It!" Why he even hates to give credit to the worker who really made the product for him!

Perhaps you will argue that after all, the man in the picture has a right. Didn't he put up the money to bulid the factory? He must have a "return on his investment," a reward for his "risk." That is what papers like the *News* and *Mirror* and *Times* and *Journal* want us to believe.

But have you ever stopped to think where his money came from in the first place?

Suppose he inherited it from his father, and his father inherited it from his grandfather. If you go back to the very beginning— my young garment worker friend—you will find that there were some workers, our fathers and grandfathers, who were being paid for three or less hours of the twelve hour days they used to work many years ago, while the grandfather of this guy in the picture took for himself what was produced during the other nine hours. In other words what the present factory owner has today is just thousands of accumulated hours of work in the form of capital that his father and his grandfather never paid our fathers and grandfathers for during the last few hundred years and more.

We must not forget that those old exploiters and slaveowners did not stop at murder—mass murder—of Indians, destroyed whole Indian civilizations, reduced them to slavery and brought other slaves in chains from far off Africa to America.

And now comes this grand, grandson of all the exploiters who ever existed, suave, manicured, without a bit of grease on his white-on-white vest, well heeled and well fed, to shout at me from his picture in a subway advertisement: "I Made It!" The gall of the guy!

The time will come when everybody will understand that you did not make it, old man. That you just took it from the workers giving them enough—just enough—to keep them going and to procreate workers like themselves for your son's factories. And the time will come here, as it has come in other lands already, when the factories and the earth on which they are built will be given back to their rightful owners: The farmers and the workers of hand and brain. They are the only ones who make anything worthwhile in this world.

50. Grandma, Please Don't Come!

Please, grandma, don't come!

I know they have sent you the airplane ticket, and a dress just your size with black and white squares all over the beautiful taffeta silk. But please, grandma, don't come!

They have sent you the photographs of your little darling grandchildren born in New York. True, you have not seen them yet. You would like to leave your tropical sun and mountains and the little rivulet bathing the base of the fence in your backyard and the tall avocado tree right by your kitchen door, just to see and embrace those darling grandchildren. But again, I say, grandma, please don't come!

I know you are not well-to-do. But you have been living on what your sons and daughters send you every month from the states. I know there is need and poverty around you And discrimination and economic and cultural oppression there. Something called imperialism sees to it that these things are not wiped out. But I think this is not the kind of letter in which I should go all out and try to explain to you why some people are so terribly interested in keeping other people poor and ignorant. Still I think I ought to tell you that the most important men and forces interested in keeping people poor and ignorant and fighting wars one against the other, have their offices in one short street in this New York to which your relatives are trying to bring you. The many companies with offices in that street and their counterparts in other great cities own the United States and of course, Puerto Rico. Eisenhower and Munoz Marin do what they ask them to do. It might sound ridiculously amazing to you. But believe me, grandma, this is nevertheless a fact. But enough of this "deep" stuff for today. All I am asking you, grandma, today, is please don't come!

Yes, it is nice here in a way. It is nice if you are young and willing and able to go down five flights of stairs two or three times a day. If you can "take it" in a crowded subway where you are squeezed in tight twice a day as if you were a cork in a bottle. It is all right in a way—and remember—I only say in a way —for young strong people. We come to New York young and leave old and tired. All the fun and joy of life extracted from us by the hurry-up machine way of living we are forced to live here. In Puerto Rico, nobody pushes you, you walk slowly as if the day had 48 hours. Persons completely unknown to you say: "Buenos Dias," (Good morning), with a reverence and a calmness in their voices that reveals centuries of a quiescent, reposed, unhurried way of life.

No matter how many photographs they sent you of Times Square at night, or the Coney Island Boardwalk, grandma, please tell them "*NO.*" A forceful, definite "*NO.*" All those things you have not seen are lots of fun. Don't misunderstand me. New York has many things that are grand. But at your age you will not really be able to enjoy them. You know what snow is? What sleet and snow is? The real physical burden of 20 additional pounds of clothing on your body when you have to go out during the winter, when you have been accustomed to two pounds of calico and muslin on your old bones? Puerto Rico's climate doesn't require any more. Grandma, please don't come!

You should see hundreds of Puerto Rican grandmas like you on a wintry snowy day, standing by the window and watching the snow fall, as Ramito our folk singer said when he came here: "Like coconut flakes falling from the sky." At the beginning snow is a novelty. But after you have seen it once or twice, you wish you were back in our Puerto Rico, looking out at your avocado tree and at the tall dignified royal palm piercing the deep blue Caribbean sky with its sheer beauty.

In Puerto Rico you will be chatting your head off in your own language with the other grandmothers. Nobody will shout at you: "Why don't you talk United States?" Or even threaten you with a beating because you are speaking Spanish. It has been done, you know. People have been killed because they are heard speaking Spanish. So, grandma, please, don't come!

You will be looking so sad, so despondent, so alone when everybody goes to work and you are left all by yourself in an apartment peering through a window at the passersby down below as they go back and forth splashing the grey, dirty, cold snow in the street and on the sidewalk!

All people, North Americans and Puerto Ricans alike, are looking to the day when they can spend the last years of their lives on a tropical isle—a paradise on earth surrounded by clear blue sea imprisoned in a belt of golden beaches. A land perfumed with nature's choicest fragrances. For many of us this is a dream that will never be realized. The boasted "American way of life" has taken out of us the best of our energies to reach that dream.

Grandma, you are there on that beautiful isle. You were born there. You have been there all your life. You now have what most people here can only dream about. Don't let sentimental letters and life-colored photographs lure you from your island, from your nation, from yourself. Grandma, please, please! DO NOT COME!

51. She Actually Pinched Me!

New York's reputation must be awful outside of New York. New York's bigness, New York's many fames don't seem to stop people living in other parts from having the most amusing notions about New York and the people who happen to live in it.

A few Sundays ago I was among the fortunate ones to be enjoying, (enjoying?) a seat in the subway. As the door opened at one of the stations a considerable group of Negro women the other side of forty came into the train. They stood by twos and fours, the whole length of the subway car asking each other questions. Evidently they were not from New York.

As the subway stopped at the next station the person sitting beside me got up and left. Two of the Negro ladies were standing in front of me. One sat in the seat just left vacant. The right thing to do was for me to get up and offer my seat to the other lady so that both of them could be sitting and talking together. This I did. I was duly thanked for it.

In order to assure them of the greatest amount of privacy for conversation that you can expect in a subway, I moved a couple of steps to the right changing my strap hanging position from my right hand to my left hand.

Just then, two other ladies belonging to the same party came over and stood in front of the two that just obtained their seats. I was in a half turned position toward them. Half jokingly, half seriously one of them asked the two sitting ladies in a whom-do-you know tone, how come they got seats while they were still standing.

"Well, somebody left the train and I sat in his seat," I heard one of the ladies explain.

"And the gentleman standing beside you got up and offered me his seat," added the other lady.

Perhaps they thought that I was not listening, for the younger of the two standing up said (in a very amazed tone): "What! a man in New York giving his seat in the subway to a lady? Impossible!" And then she added, "I want to know if he is for real." And acting on her urge, she actually pinched me on my back to see if I was "for real" and would give any sign of life. She would have been even more surprised if she new she was pinching Jesus!

It seemed to me that she went back to her home town in doubt that I was "for real"—or just a dead mummy for I did not give any sign that I had heard any part of the conversation—nor did I move or squirm when she pinched me, though I am a very ticklish fellow.

But if they could have seen my face turned away from them, they would have noticed a broad smile perilously threatening to explode into loud laughter. I was enjoying every bit of it.

New York's reputation must be awful outside of New York.

52. Looking Just a Little Forward

I am always grateful to people who return books that I have loaned to them. So very few people return books, including myself. Books have a way of remaining around. Of staying indefinitely on your shelves. You say: "I will return it next week." Next week remains next month, sometimes next year.

So when Jose dropped in that evening with my Spanish copy of Bellamy's "Looking Backward," I really felt very grateful. I knew about half a dozen persons who were ripe for reading "Looking Backward." You've got to be ripe for reading certain books. Otherwise it just doesn't make any impression. I knew several persons who were just beginning to be curious about things that count. They were getting fed up with their "best seller" popular novels and the not so eternal triangle. They were ready, for something like "Looking Backward." From there I usually advance them to Jack London's "The Iron Heel," then to Gorky's "Mother." From then on, they are more or less on the right way for basic pamphlets and the more serious theoretical works.

But these friends of mine did not know enough English to read Bellamy's book in its original language. So when Jose showed up with "El Ano Dos Mil"—"The Year Two Thousand"—the title of "Looking Backward" in Spanish-I thanked Jose heartily for returning my book.

I went to bed early to enjoy what I have found to be one of the greatest pleasures in life—reading in bed. Reading in bed is a greater pleasure than reading in the bath tub, though people who have done both don't dismiss the pleasure of reading in a bath tub as just nothing at all. After reading an article in one of the Discussion Bulletins and going through the "Speak Your Piece" letters for the day, I opened the pages of "Looking Backward." My wife did not feel like reading. She had just finished the fat six volumes in Spanish of "War and Peace" while

I just got away with the one volume digest in English before we went to see the picture. We usually share the reading lamp, placing it at the middle of the wooden backpiece of our bed. That night I took the electric lamp and put it on the floor by my side of the bed, so that the light would only hit the pages of the book I intended to read. In that way Concha could sleep in peace and I could read in bed.

I opened up "Looking Backward" at random and started reading what I have read so many times. Of course, you know the book, or somebody must have told you the story.

"Looking Backward" is the tale of one Julian West, a rich young man of leisure, born in Boston in the year 1857. Suffering from acute insomnia he ordered built a secret sleeping chamber beneath the mansion foundation where he lived with his Negro servant. When even the silence of this retreat failed to bring the desired sleep, a professional mesmerizer put him into hypnotic sleep. On the night of May 30, 1887 the professional mesmerizer put Mr. Julian West to sleep for the last time as he was to leave the city that very day. The house was burned to the ground that same night. It was not until September of the year 2,000 that the subterranean chamber was discovered by a Dr. Leete, a retired physician of Boston. Using the advanced scientific methods of that period, Julian West was readily awakened. Then followed a series of conversations between Julian West, Dr. Leete and other persons living in the United States in the year 2,000. The technical, social and economic development of our society forty years from now are described in detail. Julian West was, of course, invited to tell how The Great Transformation occurred, how the people led by the working class finally took power and transformed society from one dominated by the profit motive to one dominated by the use and service motives.

The people of the year 2,000 were quite informed about the last quarter of the 20th Century, from 1975 on. But for the third quarter of the 20th Century, especially the last ten years of this quarter they only had general information. They knew that after the Soviet Union's seventh and eighth Five-Year plans, the superiority of socialism over capitalism was so glaring that most countries were rapidly changing their form of society from capitalist to socialist. By that time Italy, France and Great Britain had been under socialist governments for some time.

The socialist minded parties, the trade unions, civic organizations and the independent voters joined together and tactfully applied their joint efforts to issues and a program in harmony with the needs of the moment and the historical development of each country had won the people of those countries for socialism.

Those living in the year 2,000 knew that after the 1958 Congressional elections when the Democratic Party lost its majority in both houses, the liberal minded element within that party started to assert itself and greatly influenced by what was happening in European and Asian countries, the liberal wing of the Democratic Party forced a left-of-center presidential ticket for the 1964 elections. The Soviet Union was practically giving away its tremendous quantities of surplus food, machinery and technical knowhow to the new African republics. China, India and the other Asian countries were cooperating on an all inclusive Asian Five Year Plan. Italy, France and Great Britain were going full blast in developing socialism. All this had a terrific impact on American public opinion. But on how this 1964 left-of-center ticket was sabotaged by the Southern Dixiecrats and the northern Democratic and Republican millionaires fearing the dominance of labor in the Democratic Party, and how this finally convinced the trade union movement—independent and CIO-AFL—to organize a labor-farmer party by 1968, the people living in the year 2,000 did not have much data.

They also had very little knowledge of the tremendous role played by the numerically small Communist Party of the United States during all the changes; how it managed to greatly influence the theoretical foundations of the new Labor-Farmer Party. From there on, tremendously strengthened by the magnificent international socialist shift, the time was not so far away when a true party of socialism, uniting all other parties of workers, farmers and independent liberals, was formed in the United States.

Julian West, as you remember in your "Looking Backward" was given the task of lecturing on the 20th Century all over the country in the year 2,000. He was invited by the president of the University of Alabama to lecture on the Ten Years of the Great Change 1965-1975.

The lecture was to take place in the beautiful new university lecture hall built the previous year, 1999, right on the very broad tree-shaded Autherine Lucy Boulevard.* Julian West felt that he had to document himself well for this series of lectures. He looked over all library and newspaper files for information on this very important period. Julian West found some bound newspaper volumes in the cellar of the main public library. The volumes said on the outsid--*Daily Worker* 1954, *Daily Worker* 1955, *Daily Worker* 1956. . . . Then Julian West started to look for the other volumes that would cover the years that he was to deal with in his lectures. But he only found one slim volume. It said *Daily Worker*, January 1957.

In the January 31, 1957 issue there was a notice in bold type boxed in the middle of the first page. It read:

> "The drop in circulation and the lack of real interest and personal sacrifice required from all workers and sympathiers of our paper, has forced us to discontinue the publication of the *Daily Worker*"

Julian West was non-plussed. The paper that would have given the whole history, round by round, of the years of the great change, had to fold up in January 1957 because of lack of circulation and financial assistance.

"Jesus! Jesus! Wake up! You know what time it is?

"You dropped your book—'Looking Backward'—on the floor— and forgot to turn off the light on your reading lamp. You must have been dreaming. Time for you to go to work at the paper!" That was Concha, my wife.

"What paper?" Then I realized I must have been dreaming, living the life of the year 2,000 with my friend Julian West.

And I was happy because our paper is still being printed. And because I was still writing for it.

---

* Named after the first Black student admitted to the University of Alabama, by a 1956 Court order. Riots resulted, and she was expelled on a technicality.

53. For the Stay-at-Homes

There are many persons who, even though they get a vacation, cannot afford to go away from the city. For a number of reasons. Or just for the one reason that seems to be so general these days.

We are not going to counsel this great fraternity of vacationers-at-home to go to the movies and console themselves with travelogues of the golden sands of the Waikiki Beach in Hawaii or read travel books about the quiet freshness of the Maine woods. Neither shall we remind these persons on vacation —but not vacationing—that we are living in a city with the greatest number of vacation attractions—famous museums, parks, monuments—though it would not be out of order to say that we might have a week well spent visiting places of interest right here in the city that we had planned to visit "some day."

But there are a number of things we could do while we are on vacation and remaining at home. For one thing we could write that letter. Remember? "That letter." Who is so punctual, so letter perfect that he has not an unanswered letter?

Yes, we could spend one morning just answering that letter that we had planned to answer for some days, or weeks . . .

We can go to visit our friends, the XYZ's. Do you remember the XYZ's? Why, it is every bit of 10 years since we visited them last. We used to play Casino with them and listen to their old sentimental song records. But, oh, their conversation was backward! They did not speak "our language." All they cared about was their Friday Night Social Club with its silly social games and chit-chat conversation.

Well, I suggest that we drop in on them one of our vacation evenings, sort of by surprise, one Friday evening, perhaps, and accompany them to their Friday Night Social Club.

Perhaps, if we keep quiet and don't try to monopolize the conversation, explaining the dialectics of this, that and the other, we might be able to learn a few things from these neighborly people.

Another pleasure in store for us is to ramble into the various sections of the city inhabited by different racial and national groups. This, of course, should not be done in the spirit of vulgar curiosity and inflated superiority. But just as if you were going to visit some family relations of our own race—the human race.

Take a few days and go to visit the Chinese and the Hungarians and the Jewish people. Go to the Puerto Rican section of Harlem. Visit the Public Market on Park Avenue, between 111th Street and 116th Street. Look at and taste some of the unfamiliar tropical fruits and products. Just walk around the neighborhood and look all around you not only with your eyes, but with your five senses, very much alert to every sound, touch and smell. Try some of the tropical refreshments. Mavi, for example, with its white foamy inviting top cap on every gallon bottle.

If you have a Puerto Rican friend, you might be invited to a Puerto Rican family. You will marvel at the cleanliness and neatness of it all, pressed as they are on all sides by the destructive power of the capitalist-made slum. These neat one and two-room homes are the ones that the photographers from the big time newspapers pass by as "not typical."

Yes, look around Negro Harlem. But on the same principle that we have already set down. Not like the idler who goes around sticking his curious nose everywhere. Not like some "social scientists" who blur their feelings, love and understanding of man with too many charts and statistics. Go to Harlem and listen to what they are saying about the student sit-ins in the South. Go to Harlem and listen.

And while you are there drop into the Schomburg Collection at 135th Street and Lenox Avenue. We may be surprised to discover the many great things we do not know about the Negro.

Some other day on our vacation we could have our lunch at Bryant Park, back of the main library at 42nd Street. There, we could eat a sandwich while listening to good music provided by the summer concert series collection of recorded music from the library.

We could also just browse for hours in the second hand book shops on Fourth Avenue from Eighth to 14th Streets. To me, one of the really great pleasures.

Or we can take a walk over the Brooklyn Bridge just as the sun is sinking its gold-crimson disc back of the far off mountains beyond the tall buildings and the river.

Or we can go to Coney Island, come out of the water and stretch ourselves on the sand. And let the kids and the adults spray you with sand as they run all over you to nowhere in particular. There is something of a feeling of equality in Coney Island, a sense of the masses and its innocent uninhibited gayety that you hardly find on any other beach.

If you go to Coney Island on a Tuesday evening to see the fireworks, take a kid with you. If you have no kids of your own, invite one of the neighborhood family across the street. There is really no fun in seeing fireworks without a kid around you to say, "AH," in wonder and delight as the darkness is pierced by the glare of the multicolored lights.

Another suggestion for your vacation idleness is to do something that you have been planning to do for years but that you have been unable to come around to do, like taking that dusty carton box from the top of that shelf to see what is really inside it. Maybe we will find in it that book we borrowed from our friend so many years ago. And the way we argued with him that we had actually returned it to him! Who knows what more is inside that box!

Or we may clean, scrub and wax the whole apartment, from the kitchen to the bedroom, so that we can brag about it all year and have something to stop the wife with when we will be accused of not doing a darn thing around the house the rest of the year.

Hope you have a nice vacation.

54. If Instead of a Professor

I have a carton at home with a label on the outside. The label reads in big crayon letters: "PARA LEER." In English this means: To Read. It should be more properly labelled: To Be Read in the Future.

It is in this carton that I place everything that I cannot immediately read in the daily papers. In that box also go the weeklies and monthlies and quarterlies that I buy but that I do not have time to tackle right away. The stuff to be read starts piling up in that carton higher and higher. Pamphlets and books, papers and magazines, one being held by the other at incredible angles looking like a paper Tower of Pisa.

The only rule followed for a printed item to land in that carton is that once there was a reason for saving it from the waste basket. It is interesting to study how the reason for saving a thing today does not seem to be reason enough for saving that same thing tomorrow. . . . Frankly speaking, when I finally find time to read some of the articles, I have forgotten the reason why I saved them in the first place.

So, one rainy Saturday or Sunday, I just tell the wife to tell the callers that I am not in, and then I proceed to shut myself in a room with the contents of my literary carton. This box has been upgraded from carrying two dozen cans of beer to treasuring between its brown walls the literary and political clippings from writers of all the Americas.

One evening last week I passed near the box. A piece of newsprint protruded further out than the others as if challenging me to liberate it from the pressure of the other publications piled over it. This I did. It was a book review in the *Herald Tribune* of Thursday, February 23, 1956. The book being reviewed was: "Louis Agassiz Fuertes: His Life Briefly Told and His Correspondence, edited by Mary Fuertes Boynton. Oxford, 317 pages, $7.50."

This time the reason why I "filed" this particular book review in my literary carton quickly came to my mind. It was a phrase used by the reviewer. He referred to Louis Agassiz Fuertes' father as "a Spanish-born professor of civil engineering at Cornell." It would have been more accurate if the reviewer would have written that the famous bird painter and ornithologist's father was "a Puerto Rican born professor of Civil Engineering at Cornell University." For Dr. Esteban Antonio Fuertes was born on May 10, 1838 at San Juan, Puerto Rico.

It never fails. When the person in question has been involved in any recriminatory act and he happens to be a Puerto Rican, the fact of his country of origin is conspicuously printed and recorded in all the newspapers. But when the person has done or is doing something worthwhile, the papers seem to conveniently forget if she or he is a Puerto Rican or of Puerto Rican descent. It seems as if the newspapers hate to destroy the false picture of the Puerto Rican that these very same papers have helped to imprint in the collective patterns of thinking that go to form public opinion.

We expect this sort of thing from the cheap tabloids. But when this tendency is reflected in the so-called better papers, we have reason to become surprised if not alarmed.

Dr. Esteban Antonio Fuertes, the father of Louis Agassiz Fuertes, was educated in the Puerto Rican schools and later in the famous University of Salamanca, Spain, from which he graduated as a Doctor of Philosophy . He then came to the Rensselaer Polytechnic Institute from which he graduated with an engineering degree in 1861 at the age of 33.

He returned to Puerto Rico, where he was made Director of Public Works for the western part of the island.

Dr. Esteban Antonio Fuertes came back to the United States where for six years he was first assistant engineer and later engineer in charge of the works of the famous Croton Aqueduct that provides water for the City of New York. According to the Dictionary of American Biography, vol. VII, page 52, published by Scribners, Dr. Fuertes left his chief engineer position at the Croton Aqueduct, "because his sense of honesty and professional ethics would not allow him to acquiesce in the practices of the Tweed ring."

So, there you have it. Dr. Esteban Antonio Fuertes—a Puerto Rican—contributing to the material development of New York and heightening the level of political honesty and integrity of this city, almost 100 years before Marcantonio.

From 1870 to 1871 this Puerto Rican engineer was sent as the director of the official expedition that went to explore the possibilities of an isthmic canal through Nicaragua to unite the Atlantic and Pacific Oceans.

In 1873 Dr. Fuertes accepted the position of dean of the department of Civil Engineering at Cornell University. Again let us copy from the Dictionary of American Biography. Referring to Dr. Fuertes, this reference work says: "Perhaps it was his insistence on a judicious combination of practice and theory which was his greatest contribution to the educational methods of the time."

Dr. Fuertes resigned after 30 years at Cornell on November 1902, because of ill health. On January 16, 1903, Dr. Esteban Antonio Fuertes died.

This is the "Spanish-born" professor, whom the New York Herald Tribune book reviewer mentions as the father of a great American bird painter and ornithologist.

We do not think that it is too much to ask of the papers that when they write about a Puerto Rican who happened to have done something good to please mention the fact that he is a Puerto Rican.

Mentioning the many good things done by Puerto Ricans and the Puerto Rican people as a whole will help to destroy their enemies.

55. A Puerto Rican in New York

"Why did you come to New York?" That question has been asked of me at least one hundred times during the over forty-odd years I have been living in this city. I find for one thing that the reasons for my coming cannot be just stated in a few words. That, as everything else, these reasons have a beginning, a process of development and an end that has not been reached yet. So, without trying to answer the question directly I will try to give you something of the background and a few observations that I made in my childhood and my youth. Observations—deeper and broader—that I am still making.

Out of that jumble of facts and feelings, glimpses of life and thinking on Puerto Rico and the Puerto Ricans and their coming to the United States in ever larger numbers, you yourself will discover why I did come to New York. Why we Puerto Ricans are coming today to the many cities and rural areas in the United States.

●　　●　　●

I still remember the day the school gave me that fat history book: *A History of the United States.* It was around 1915. I was in the 8th grade at elementary school. As kids do all over the world I started looking at the maps and pictures and getting acquainted with the moon-looking face of George Washington and the solemn figure of Abraham Lincoln. Almost by accident I came to discover a phrase in one of the documents at the end of the book.

The phrase opened the document. And that phrase stuck with me all day like one of those musical phrases of a nameless song that keeps coming up in the sound of your whistling again and again, sometimes for hours. That phrase was: "We, the people

197

of the United States . . ." I did not read any more of the document. That was enough. It was great! You and I and all those
people whom we have studied in the flat cream-colored geography, the people who picked cotton in Alabama, and wheat in the
Dakotas, and grapes in California. All those who manufactured Singer machines in New Jersey and shoes in Boston, and built the great
big ships in Brooklyn and Philadelphia shipyards. All of them
together with myself and my father, the Puerto Rican baker,
and the sugar worker in the sugar plantation in Puerto Rico—
"We are the people of the United States." Why, that would
be great if it was true! That reproduction of what was undoubtedly
in the original old document said so. We belonged.

I went home from school with that phrase on my lips. Repeating it over and over again.—"We the people of the United
States." And I accented the phrase with the pounding of my
feet over the centuries-old cobblestones of the streets in old San
Juan. We-the-people-of-the-United-States.

My 8th grade teacher was a six-foot Montanan. Mr. Whole
was his name. A fading smile always on his lips. One day he was
sitting on the wide porch of the YMCA. (For the construction
of this building we in school were politely obliged to bring in a
quarter as a contribution.) Mr. Whole hailed me from the
porch. He invited me to play a game of checkers. I sat in front
of him, the checker board between us, ready to start the game.
Out came somebody in authority. He informed Mr. Whole that
I could not play there with him as I did not belong to the white
race. Mr. Whole said not a word and the game, not yet
started, ended.

That incident put me to thinking. In this "we the people"
phrase that I admired so much, were there first and secondary
people? Were there other gradations and classifications not only
because of race but because of money or social position?

Reading and life itself taught me the truth: That there were
classifications and divisions. Yes, that there were classes. The
rich and the poor. The sugar planter and the sugar peon. And
I was surprised to discover that the rich Puerto Rican sugar planter
and the rich American investor belonged to the same clubs, played

golf and danced and dined together. And that they together despised and exploited the Puerto Rican masses.

Still in short pants, I started going to Federation Hall (Federacion Libre de los Trabajadores) and I began to read *Justicia* (Justice) and *Union Obrera* (Workers Union). I changed from writing poor sonnets to reading good pamphlets.

I found that the Americans did not come to Puerto Rico because of the altruistic and democratic reasons that General Miles gave in his proclamation, when the Yankees invaded Puerto Rico. I found that a race to dominate the markets of the world was on. This race was called "Imperialism." The United States was just getting into this race around 1898. I further learned that ever since the Americans came into Puerto Rico our land that produced varied products for everyday meals was converted into a huge sugar factory with owners living far away—caring absolutely nothing about the standards of living of the broad agricultural masses comprising two-thirds of the Puerto Rican population. The sun-up to sun-down hours of work under the burning tropical sun cutting cane were jokingly paid at a dollar and fifty cents a day. Then six months of "invernazo"—which means that sugar, being a seasonal industry, the workers were without work for more than six months.

As if I had never seen it before, I discovered that all my school books, except of course Spanish grammar, were written in English. It would be just as if you New Yorkers or Californians discovered one good morning that all your childrens' books, but the one on English grammar were written in Spanish.

I opened up my eyes as if for the first time. Right by the big mansion of the sugar plantation owner or the comfortable house of the overseer, I started noticing the hundreds of old crudely made peasant huts and slums of the worst kind, with thousands of people starving in them.

The workers and the cigar makers taught me—they gave me pamphlets and papers to read—they told me that we were a colony —a sort of storage house for cheap labor and a market for "seconds" (cheap industrial goods). That we Puerto Ricans were a part of a great colonialism system. And that not until colonialism was wiped out and full independence given to Puerto Rico would the conditions under which we were living be remedied.

I suddenly realized that there was no future for a young man in Puerto Rico, but the future of the sugar cane field, with starvation wages. The future of an upward struggle with great odds against you. Today I realize after forty years of experience that there was another future: The pleasure of fighting hard and furiously against the conditions imposed by the colony.

I came to New York to poor pay, long hours, terrible working conditions, discrimination even in the slums and in the poor paying factories where the bosses very dexterously pitted Italians against Puerto Ricans and Puerto Ricans against American Negroes and the Jews. Somehow in New York, I did not seem to find the pot of gold at the end of the rainbow that I was so sure I would find in my dreams while in Puerto Rico. The same American trusts that exploited us in Puerto Rico were in control in New York. Trusts— the tangible expression of Imperialism and colonial exploitation— were not only exploiting the Puerto Ricans in New York but the other various national minorities and workers in general as well.

Why are the reactionary papers against Puerto Ricans coming to New York? Why do the reactionary forces describe the Puerto Ricans in the worst light they can imagine? Simply because they know that colonial conditions of exploitation and the cry for their economic, social and political independence made them progressive. That their American idol was and still is Vito Marcantonio. That as progressives with the right to vote as American citizens they are a very real danger to the reactionary forces in the United States, the destroyers of civil rights, the red-baiters and thought controllers—that they are a real menace to the Un-Americans now temporarily in power in Washington.

The Puerto Ricans are getting into the unions, and progressive fraternal, civil and political organizations. They are not only looking and getting unity but are cooperating with other national groups and progressive forces in America today.

The Puerto Ricans in New York are realizing that somehow there is an affinity between the phrases "We the people" and "Arise, you workers," and are fast adapting themselves to the best fighting and democratic traditions of this country. So you can see why some people don't like them to come to the United States.

Well, you might say that was forty years ago. You might say that in forty years things might have changed. I say that fundamentally speaking things have not changed. We are still a colony rationalized with the high sounding name of a Commonwealth. Notwithstanding the objective industrial development, our economy is totally dependent on that of the United States. The question of a final political status for Puerto Rico has not been solved yet.

True that the 500-acre law*—that had not been enforced since it was enacted in 1901—is enforced today. That there is a Popular Democratic Party that has done planning and enacted social legislation. But it is also true that the tariff and coastwise laws that oblige Puerto Rico to buy almost exclusively in the highest market in the world are still a reality. That is why I say that colonialism is still there.

Colonialism made me leave Puerto Rico about forty years ago. Colonialism with its concomitants, agricultural slavery, monoculture, absentee ownership and rank human exploitation are making the young Puerto Ricans of today come in floods to the United States, if only for a few months to work in the equally exploited agricultural fields.

For the ones that are here in greater New York—six hundred thousand strong—let us show them that there are millions of people that are struggling to take the country away from the trusts that exploit Puerto Rico and the United States alike. Yes, that there are millions of persons to whom that phrase I read many years ago—"We the people"—means what it says, that we are ready to fight for lower prices, more housing, for a progressive people's government and for peace for "We the people of the United States in order to form a more perfect union."

Regardless of the American sugar planters in Puerto Rico, nobody is going to make me believe that that phrase may not be true.

---

*A law forbidding any corporation in Puerto Rico to own more than 500 acres of land. This was of course circumvented by the organization of holding companies and other "legal" means by the corporations.

When that phrase is realized in its totality, Puerto Ricans will have the right to choose the form of government they really want. And when that opportunity comes I will choose independence. I have studied and weighed all the choices. Independence is the way that will provide for everything—material and spiritual—for the people of Puerto Rico. Independence and socialism. Socialism and independence.

As I see things moving in the whole world, among the broad masses and socialist-minded forces in the United States, and among the Puerto Rican nation, including potential forces within all its political parties, independence for Puerto Rico will come sooner than you think.

Cuba and Puerto Rico are the two wings of a bird
Lola Rodriguez de Tio